David Andersen is a passionate man about prayer and the Word of God. Within a few pages you will begin to experience his passion, and by the end it will be your passion as well. But it won't be a passion for prayer in general, but very specifically for the political leaders of our nation and the nations of the world. When the church is ignited with this passion, God just might bring revival through political leaders. That is my prayer for our nation, and this book has been a stimulus backed by the promises of God. IN GOD WE TRUST!

Jim Young
President
Capitol Commission

David Andersen's book, Christ's Kingdom Commission is a scholarly and well-written analysis of the Biblical strategy of sharing the faith by focusing on reaching leaders in capital cities. The book has certainly been an encouragement for our ministry's work of reaching Members of Congress with the gospel.

Dr. George Roller
Executive Director
D. James Kennedy Center for Christian Statesmanship

Weary of all of the attacks on our political leaders from both sides, not only by the news outlets, but also by conservative Christians? David Andersen has a better idea... He carefully and exegetically surveys both the Old and New Testaments to demonstrate that our responsibility as Christians to our civil leaders is two-fold: (1) Pray for them; and (2) Take every opportunity to preach God's Word to them. Though brief, this is a significant book that Christians need to read.

Larry Pettegrew, Th. D.
Dean of Shepherds Theological Seminary
Cary, NC

FOREWORD BY
JOHN MACARTHUR

CHRIST'S
KINGDOM
COMMISSION

THE STRATEGIC IMPORTANCE
OF EVANGELISM TO
"KINGS AND ALL IN AUTHORITY"

DAVID J. ANDERSEN

Published by:

Leadership Library
P.O. Box 1063
Graham, NC 27253

LEADERSHIP
LIBRARY

ISBN: 978-1-629460-09-3

Christ's Kingdom Commission

© 2013, David Jonathan Andersen, Author. All rights reserved.

Cover design: Jeremy Bennett, kalosgrafx.com

© Leadership Library, 2014. All rights reserved. Leadership Library an English imprint of Publicaciones Faro de Gracia.

First edition: printed in USA, 2014

This book is gratefully dedicated to:

The Speaker of the House of Delegates of Virginia

The Honorable Bill Howell

Who has faithfully taught a Bible study with the Virginia legislators since 1993, beginning with only three others, Congressman Randy Forbes, Governor Bob McDonnell and Virginia Supreme Court Justice Bill Mims, and who currently still teaches the Bible study among our Virginia legislators

And

the Congressman representing the Fourth District of Virginia

The Honorable Randy Forbes

For his commitment to prayer in starting and continuing to lead the Congressional Prayer Caucus in the United States Capitol since 2005

Both of these statesmen are personally fulfilling
Christ's Kingdom Commission
through prayer and the ministry of the Word (Acts 6:4)

CONTENTS

Acknowledgements

My gratitude is expressed first and foremost to the King of Kings and Lord of Lords for the unusual manifestation of His providence in calling me to this ministry through this very study in His Word, and giving me the privilege of serving our Virginia leaders. His providential hand has been unusually present in the entire process of bringing this work to fruition. His hand has been seen in so many ways that this page cannot possibly contain the entire list of details.

My appreciation goes to all of those who have partnered with us in this ministry over the last twelve years in prayer and support, as legislators, donors, sponsors, event directors, coordinators, decorators, photographers, videographers, volunteers, participants, mail helpers and pastors/elders who long to see our leaders transformed. I am particularly thankful for those in my home church for their faithfulness in sending our leaders note cards, informing our leaders of our prayers for them and those in our church family who have been so encouraging, embracing us and our vision to win our leaders for Christ.

My gratitude goes especially to Wayne at Leadership Library who believed in this project and vision from the beginning, who has helped so diligently on the manuscript, and who has been so professional in every part of producing this publication.

My deepest love and appreciation goes to my Beloved, Eunjoo, my treasured partner in life and ministry. Without her by my side I would have never been free to seek the Lord in prayer and His Word or minister to our leaders as the Lord has privileged me to do. My gratitude goes as well to all of my family who have supported this project with their prayers and encouragement.

What partnership and gratitude is mine for all the Capitol Commission team, the Board members, all in the national office and each of those in our twenty two states who patiently encourage the weakest among us, and who are doing such a strategic work in fulfilling Christ's Kingdom Commission.

My great appreciation also goes to my friend who prays for me daily, who read this book many times (encouraging me to excellency), and who generously provided MacArthur Study Bibles for all of our legislators in the United States Congress this year.

Finally, my overwhelming gratitude goes to my former Pastor, and Seminary President, Dr. John MacArthur, for his example and dedication to prayer and ministry of the Word over the years, and for his gracious willingness to write the forward for this work. My appreciation also goes to Pat Rotisky, John Bates and especially Phil Johnson at Grace Community Church for their help in speedily expediting the process of acquiring the forward.

Christ's
Kingdom
Commission

by

David J. Andersen

FOREWORD

The apostle Paul knew that warfare was a fitting metaphor for his entire life and ministry—and he urged other Christians to think the same way. He told his protégé, Timothy, *"Suffer hardship with me, as a good soldier of Christ Jesus"* (2 Timothy 2:3). He described his co-laborers as fellow soldiers (Philippians 2:25; Philemon 2). They were engaged side-by-side in a never-ending battle, and Paul never took a rest from it. Thus as he neared the end of his earthly life, Paul said, *"I have fought the good fight, I have finished the course, I have kept the faith; in the future there is laid up for me the crown of righteousness, which the Lord, the righteous Judge, will award to me on that day"* (2 Timothy 4:7-8).

It wasn't that Paul relished fighting or went looking for trouble. On the contrary, because of his effectiveness as a herald of truth, the enemy sought him out and relentlessly attacked. Paul's whole life was filled with conflict and persecution—much of it at the hands of Roman officials. His ministry was contemporaneous with the political career of Nero, one of the most brutal and demented men who ever sat on the emperor's throne. Nero hated everything

Paul stood for, and he attempted to wipe out the church in that first generation after Pentecost. He was not alone. Rome's whole political machinery was dominated by evil men whose official policies were anti-Christian.

You might think, then, that Paul saw the Roman government as the enemy with whom he was at war. But he emphatically stated otherwise: *"Our struggle is not against flesh and blood, but against the rulers, against the powers, against the world forces of this darkness, against the spiritual forces of wickedness in the heavenly places"* (Ephesians 6:12). The enemy was Satan and his demonic minions, not Nero and the Roman Senate.

The apostle's strategy was therefore nothing like conventional warfare. He wrote, *"The weapons of our warfare are not of the flesh, but divinely powerful for the destruction of fortresses. We are destroying speculations and every lofty thing raised up against the knowledge of God, and we are taking every thought captive to the obedience of Christ"* (2 Corinthians 10:4-5).

Notice: what Paul describes there is not a war for territory, political status, or material resources. It is an ideological battle. It is a war for the truth, and the goal is liberation of minds and hearts, including the hearts and minds of those evil Roman rulers who were so zealously persecuting the church.

Weapon number one in the apostolic arsenal against evil government policies was *prayer*—not sabotage, lobbying, boycotts, protests, or other forms of political agitation. Furthermore, what Paul sought from God was not the destruction of Nero and his government, but his well-being, and specifically his salvation. Paul made such prayer a mandate for the whole church: *"First of all, then, I urge that entreaties and prayers, petitions and thanksgivings, be made on behalf of all men, for kings and all who are in authority, so that we may lead a tranquil and quiet life in all godliness and dignity. This is good and acceptable in the sight of God our Savior, who desires all men to be saved and to come to the knowledge of the truth"* (1 Timothy 2:1-4).

This book skillfully unpacks and carefully examines that mandate and its implications. After several decades of failed evangelical attempts to influence culture by political means, here is a better way. It is the biblical answer to the question of what the church's duty is with respect to hostile governments and anti-Christian rulers. I'm thankful for the painstaking work David Andersen has done on this project. I know you will be challenged, blessed, and encouraged as you read.

John MacArthur

Introduction

A Surprising Discovery

Where should I begin in order to fulfill the requirement? My mind raced to find a theme that would capture the attention of my audience and fill the time. The first requirement of my seminary preaching class was to preach an entire sermon introducing I Thessalonians before expositing the first verse. Thinking through many possibilities, I settled on discovering the reason why Paul had chosen the city of Thessalonica to evangelize. All the prior cities could be studied for clues as well as Thessalonica. Was it possible that Paul had a clear strategy that drew him to the cities he evangelized?

Walking through the book of Acts with Paul and Barnabas and then Paul and Silas, there seemed to be a pattern developing: Paul was going to major cities. That strategy seemed to work – until arriving at the city immediately preceding Thessalonica. There Paul evangelized Philippi, a city smaller than Ampiphilos and Appolonia, cities through which Paul had traveled without saying a word. Upon leaving Philippi, he went on to Thessalonica. So to my dismay, my "large city" paradigm floated like a small boat with a large hole.

Having expended my time for study, the message had to be delivered. Lacking a strategy, my message was missing its uniting theme, and certainly failed to hit the mark. I made an attempt to create interest in the evangelized cities, but failing to find a unifying strategy, it seemed everyone was disappointed, no one more than myself. Surely the man who was so successful that he was accused by his enemies in Thessalonica of turning the world upside down, would have only known this kind of conquest by having a strategy to guide his efforts. This concept remained in the back of my mind as a mystery begging to be solved.

About a year later, when introduced to a ministry that would later lead me to Capitol Commission, the solution to this mystery suddenly flashed upon my mind. I remembered that many of the cities of Paul's ministry were capital cities! I couldn't wait to get home and review them all one more time. There was no sleep that night as the discovery of Paul's commission and the cities he evangelized unfolded in my study, clearly revealing his strategy. As though it were yesterday, I remember telling my wife the next morning that I never dreamed that I could be called to a specific ministry solely through a study of God's missionary strategy contained within the Scriptures. Here presented in this book is the more mature fruit of that initial study, representing the evidence mined from Scripture and history regarding Christ's Kingdom Commission.

The purpose of this work, then, is to show how God is strategically bringing His name and His redemption to all the nations, perhaps best highlighted in the life of Daniel, one of the greatest statesman in the Bible who was used by God to win the king who required the citizenry of his entire world empire to *"fear and tremble before the God of Daniel; For He is the living God and enduring forever, and His kingdom is one which will not be destroyed, and His dominion will be forever."* (Daniel 6:25-26)

The Commissions of Christ

As in the case of the presentation of the gospel throughout God's Word, Christ's commissions are first given in seed form, and then developed throughout the rest of Scripture.

The glorious gospel of Jesus Christ begins in seed form in Genesis 3:15: *"I will put enmity between you and the woman, and between your offspring and her offspring; he shall bruise your head, and you shall bruise his heal."* That theme continues to be revealed throughout the Old Testament until it grows into the clearer revelation of God's Suffering Servant in Isaiah 52-53. Finally, the revelation of the vicarious atonement of Christ for our sins upon the cross comes to a complete crescendo in the New Testament.

Similarly, the four commissions of Jesus Christ in the New Testament begin with an initial command to His Apostles and His Church in the Great Commission found in Matthew 28:19-20: "*All authority has been given to Me in heaven and on earth. Go therefore and make disciples of all the nations, baptizing them in the name of the Father and the Son and the Holy Spirit, teaching them to observe all that I commanded you; and lo, I am with you always, even to the end of the age.*" It is restated in Acts 1:8, and later more clearly revealed to Paul in Acts 9:15, until it climaxes to its fullest expression in 1 Timothy 2:1-4. In addition to the unquestioned mandate of evangelism, the common connection in all four commissions is an emphasis on evangelizing leaders.

The First Commission of Christ (The Great Commission- Matthew 28:19-20)

Christ several times surprised His apostles after His resurrection, instantly materializing in their midst. But there was one appointment that Jesus made with them in which they expected Him to appear – the mountaintop in the Gospel of Matthew. It had been specifically designated before and after His death (Mat.26:32, 28:7, 16). (For any attorney reading this book, this strategic appointment provides another evidence for the most proven event in the history of the world, the Resurrection![1]) On this occasion, Jesus proclaimed His universal authority revealing the divine power behind the Great Commission of Matthew 28:19-20. Since this would have been the only sure opportunity to see the Risen Lord, most likely over 500 were there to hear this commission (1 Cor.15:6).

4

John MacArthur, in agreement with many other commentators, says of this passage:

"If a Christian understands all the rest of the Gospel of Matthew but fails to understand this closing passage, he has missed the point of the entire book. This passage is the climax and major focal point, not only of this gospel, but of the entire New Testament."[2]

The emphasis in the Great Commission is on the only verb, "*disciple*" and sole direct object: "*all the nations.*" Griffith Thomas, one of the founders of Dallas Theological Seminary, may be the clearest in presenting the significance of this direct object:

"The commission embraces *whole nations* rather than indicating individuals among them.[emphasis added]"[3]

John Piper argues extensively against an "individual" interpretation, not only in the New Testament, but also from the Old Testament. Having researched thoroughly every verse which includes the phrase, "*all the nations*" he states, "the phrase *panta ta ethne* occurs in the Greek Old Testament some 100 times and virtually never carries the meaning of Gentile individuals but always carries the meaning '*all the nations.*'"[4] If it is true that the command to "*disciple all the nations*" is not referring to individuals but to whole nations, then discipling whole nations requires a strategy that must include those who influence and direct the whole nation, the leaders of the nations.

The Second Commission of Christ (The Commission to Capitals - Acts 1:8)

The restatement of the Great Commission of Christ in Acts 1:8 adds greater light to this leadership strategy of evangelism as Jesus commanded His Apostles in his last words just before He ascended: *"But you will receive power when the Holy Spirit has come upon you; and you will be My witnesses in Jerusalem and in all Judea, and Samaria, and to the end of the earth."* In the use of the term, "discipling all nations", what is *"Jerusalem"* in regard to the nation of Israel? It is the capital. They had been told no less than four times that they were to stay in *"Jerusalem"* (Lk 24:47, 49; Acts 1:4, 1:8). It was strategic that they begin in their capital city of Jerusalem. They were then to evangelize *"all Judea"* where most of the leadership lived which would influence the nation. Galilee, where Jesus spent most of His time in ministry is not even included in this commission. Instead, they were to go to the next closest capital, Samaria, and continue that strategy, *"to the end of the earth"*, a phrase often used in the Old Testament to refer to imperial capitals.

The Third Commission of Christ (the Commission of Paul, the Missionary)

Saul saw a light far greater than the sun when he met the risen Lord. His appearance was so bright that Saul suffered temporary blindness while waiting for his commission from Christ through Ananias. If one might question the strategic emphasis on leaders in the first two commissions, the direct and personal commission to Paul, Christ's primary missionary Apostle to the Gentiles in fulfillment of the Great Commission, leaves no room for doubt: "*He is a chosen instrument of mine to carry My name before the Gentiles and **kings** and the children of Israel.*" (Acts 9:15). The "*kings*" in the third and fourth commissions has an undeniable emphasis on leaders. And where will Saul, later Paul, find these three people groups in his commission, "*Gentiles, kings, children of Israel?*" In no other place than capital cities. As we will see, this strategy of winning leaders and capital evangelism is revealed both in his name change and in the cities of Paul's travels.

Fourth Commission of Christ (the Climax of the Commissions)

This crescendo of emphasis on evangelizing political leadership continues to gain clarity through the commissions, finding its full and final development in 1 Timothy 2:1-4:

> "*Therefore I exhort **first of all** that supplications, prayers, intercessions, and giving of thanks be made for all men, **For kings and all who are in authority**, that we may lead a quiet and peaceable life in all godliness and reverence. For this is good and acceptable in the sight of God our **Savior**, who desires all men to be **saved** and to **come to the knowledge of the truth**.*" (NKJV)

Here, the Spirit-inspired Paul passes on his commission to the Church universal with a clear double emphasis on leaders. This concluding commission is found in the singular book in the New Testament with the expressed purpose of ordering biblical conduct in the Church, "*the house of the living God, the pillar and ground of truth*" (1 Tim.3:15).

1 Timothy 2:1-4 deals with at least seven major essentials for the Church (in expositional order):

1) The Necessity of Prayer in the Church
2) The Clear Commissions for the Church
3) The Responsibility of the Church to the Government
4) The Strategic Mission of the Church
5) The Effective Means of Peace for the Church and Liberty for the gospel
6) The Leadership Model of Evangelism for the Church
7) The Passion of God to save the Lost through His Church

This text also raises four important questions, each answered by a chapter in this book:

1) Why is prayer such an important priority of God for His Church in the evangelization of the nations?
2) How does the development of the commissions in God's Word emphasize the strategic evangelism of political leaders?
3) What is the importance of prayer for "*kings and all who are in authority,*" as a God-given means of peace for the Church in its relationship to government, in order to enjoy freedom for the gospel?

4) What does God Himself say about His passion for the salvation of political leaders and for religious freedom to spread the gospel?

Let us find the answers in God's Word, anticipating its purest pleasure and richest profit. Our purpose is not simply to convince the reader of the importance of ministering to our political leaders, but to stimulate pastors and the people of God worldwide to understand this priority and become strategically involved in the evangelism of leaders through God's prescribed power sources: prayer and ministry of the Word. Additionally, by focusing on the relationship of the church to government, we hope to encourage the peace of the Church throughout the world facing persecution, and the means to freedom for the gospel. This brief work will focus expositionally on the final and climactic commission of Christ to His Church found in 1 Timothy 2:1-4, drawing from the full scope of God's Word.

Endnotes

1 The Bible study covering the resurrection as the most proven event in the history of the world is on our Capitol Commission website, www.capitolcom.org. Click on "State Ministries" at the top, then the state of Virginia, "Bible Studies" at the top left, "2012," "May 17, 2012 Matthew 28:11-15, The Leaders' Lie Proving the Resurrection." http://www.capitolcom.org/virginia/studies/943/2012/05/17/mt-28-11-15-the-leaders-lie-proving-the-resurrection.

2 John MacArthur, *The MacArthur New Testament Commentary* (Chicago: Moody Press, 1989), 329.

3 Griffith Thomas, *Outline Studies in Matthew* (Grand Rapids, Michigan: Kregel Publications, 1985), 464.

4 John Piper, *Let the Nations Be Glad!* (Grand Rapids, Michigan: Baker Books, 1993), 181.

In the context of Christ's kingdom commission and the discipling of the nations, prayer takes a "first of all" priority for the Church and for the believer.

FIRST OF ALL

Prayer: A First Priority

Imagine that you lived in the days of the early apostles, and you had been given the commission of Christ to evangelize all the nations for the dominion of His kingdom, where would you begin? There was no mass media, no internet communication, no real postal system, no iPads, cell phones, or computers, not even electricity available. And what if there were no modern forms of transportation, no airplanes, no cars, no trains, no propeller driven boats, not even an engine or gasoline? What if there were no nooks, publications or printed books.

And what if the world was under the scourge of merciless dictators who ruled with little concern for the welfare of the populace? If you and your church were required to win that world to Christ in a lifetime, how would you do it? What would your strategy look like? And what if you knew that you and your church would suffer intense persecution, and many would be killed while trying to fulfill this one essential task, would it change your strategy?

This was the commission given to the Apostles. Yet without all our modern means of communication, transportation, publication, or political freedoms, they powerfully fulfilled the Great Commission in their own lifetime. Albert Barns tells us:

> "Within the space of *thirty years* after the death of Christ, the gospel had been carried to all the parts of the civilized, and to no small portion, of the uncivilized world. Its progress and its triumphs were not concealed. Its great transactions were not "done in a corner". It had been preached in the most splendid, powerful, and enlightened cities; churches were already founded in Jerusalem, Antioch, Corinth, Ephesus, Philippi, and at Rome. The gospel had spread in Arabia, Asia Minor, Greece, Macedon, Italy, and Africa. It had assailed the most mighty existing institutions; it had made its way over the formidable barriers; it had encountered the most deadly and most malignant; it had traveled to the capital, and had secured such a hold even in the imperial city as to make it certain that it would finally overturn the established religion and seat itself on the ruins of paganism. Within thirty years it had settled the point that it would overturn every bloody altar, close every pagan temple, bring under its influence men of office, rank, and power and that 'the banners of the faith would soon stream from the palaces of the Caesars.'" [5]

So how did they accomplish this amazing feat? They followed the priority found in this divine commission: *"First of All"*.

In the context of Christ's kingdom commission and the discipling of the nations, prayer takes a "first of all" priority for the church and for the believer. Paul, recognizing the tsunami of persecution approaching the Church, passes on his commission received from Christ himself. Here he provides the divine means to overcome through a fourfold emphasis on prayer as a first priority: "*Therefore I exhort first of all that supplications, prayers, intercessions, and giving of thanks be made for all men, for kings and all who are in authority*" (1 Timothy 2:1-2, NKJV). This text provides what may be one of the clearest passages in Scripture on the priority of prayer.[6]

"*Therefore*" (ουν) specifically points back to the theme of the previous chapter emphasizing a sincere love: "*the goal of our instruction is **love** from a pure heart and a good conscience and a sincere faith*" (1 Timothy 1:5). It also points back to Paul's transformation from a life of hatred and persecution as "*formerly a blasphemer, **a persecutor**, and **injurious***" (1 Timothy 1:13, NKJV) to a passionate, world-evangelizing Apostle. Additionally Paul has just "*handed over to Satan*" Hymenaeus and Alexander because they were diverting the church from the necessary demonstration of love through their foolish and unnecessary conflicts over trivialities (1 Timothy 1:4, 6). Paul concludes chapter one with the charge to Timothy to resist those who through petty contention and conflict disrupt the love and harmony of the church. Thus, this priority of prayer is given as a clear fulfillment of the primary goal of his instruction: love. Love is the foundation for his important exhortation to prayer.

Consider carefully the strength of His first expression in the original text, "*I exhort:*" Paul does not use παραινεω, meaning "to tell of, speak of, recommend," hence "to advise, exhort, warn."[7] Neither does he use προτρεπω, meaning, "to turn forward, propel (προ-before, τρεπω-to turn), thus, "to impel morally, to urge forward, encourage."[8] Instead, God uses the strongest yet the most intimate and loving verb available as an exhortation: παρακαλεω, meaning "to call a person" (παρα-to the side, καλεω-to call) "to call on, entreat; to admonish, exhort, to urge."[9] It is the word primarily used to describe the Holy Spirit as the Paraclete, in His loving authority in the heart of the believer. This exhortation reflects the love and authority of God Himself.

Most importantly, this exhortation to prayer is given first priority, "***first of all***" (προτος παντων). This word not only relates to time (do it first), but especially to its immense weight of importance. Jesus best defined this word in Matthew 22:37-38, when he said, "*This is the great and **first** commandment.*" The Pharisees had only asked for the "*great*" commandment but He answered, "*You shall love the LORD your God with all your heart and with all your soul and with all your mind. This is the great and **first** commandment.*"

The first word describing prayer, "*Supplications,*" presents a great privilege. This verb had evolved from its initial meaning, "to chance upon," to later signify the tremendous opportunity, "to have an audience with a king." Long after Paul's day, the word became a regular term for a petition to a superior, and in the papyri it was constantly used of any writing addressed to the king.[10]

The word "*Prayers*" goes beyond supplications to signify the greatest privilege possible, and is only used of petitioning the King of the Universe. Although earthly kings can grant requests involving their sphere of control, only our great God controls the entire universe with unlimited power. And although this word is sometimes used of private prayers, its primary context is public prayers And these prayers are especially to be made for government officials. The first use of this word in the New Testament is the passage where Jesus specifically commands His disciples to "*love your enemies and **pray** for those who persecute you*" (Matthew 5:44, see also Luke 6:28).

"*Intercessions*" are similar to "*supplications*" in petitioning the King,[11] but this word includes the implication of love and interested concern by interceding on behalf of someone else.

"*Thanksgiving*" may require an attitude adjustment, and is the only word of the four that speaks of the **content** of our prayer and the spirit with which we approach God, especially for those in authority over us. Colossians 4:2 tells us: "*Continue steadfastly in prayer, being watchful in it with thanksgiving.*" This command specifically guides us in how we are to pray both for ourselves and others, and how we are to address God when we enter His throne room of grace. "*Enter His gates with thanksgiving, and His courts with praise! Give thanks to Him, bless His name!*" (Psalm 100:4)

Thus, for the advancement of His kingdom, the Church is exhorted to appeal to God's throne as a first priority. This includes a unique recognition of His authority and His special concern for those in authority. The grateful intercession for "*all who are in authority*" over us is His divine means of furthering His kingdom.

What is the basis of this fourfold emphasis on prayer, making it a first priority of the Church?

I. Intercessory Prayer Simultaneously Fulfills the Two Greatest Commandments

When Jesus was asked regarding the greatest commandment, "*He said to him, 'You shall love the LORD your God with all your heart and with all your soul, and with all your mind. This is the great and first commandment. And a second is like it: You shall love your neighbor as yourself. On these two commandments depend all the Law and the Prophets*" (Matthew 22:34-40). Intercessory prayer for others **directly** fulfills both of these commandments simultaneously.

To love God is to love as He loves and love what He loves: "*But God shows His love for us, in that while we were still sinners, Christ died for us."* (Romans 5:8) He loves sinners, and more specifically sinners who were His enemies. (Romans 5:10) He tells us in Matthew 5:43-48 that we prove our sonship by doing the same,

> *"You have heard that it was said, 'You shall love your neighbor and hate your enemy.' But I say to you, love your enemies and* **pray** *for those who persecute you,* **so that you may be sons of your Father who is in heaven***; for He makes His sun rise on the evil and on the good, and sends rain on the just and on the unjust. For if you love those who love you, what reward do you have? Do not even the tax collectors do the same? And if you greet only your brothers, what more are you doing than others? Do not even the Gentiles do the same? You therefore must be perfect, just as your heavenly Father is perfect."* (emphasis added)

According to Christ, love for our enemies is first demonstrated by our prayer for them. The love that reveals the love of the Father and demonstrates His image in us is a love that prays for our enemies, even requesting the Father's blessing upon them. This type of love is a powerful means of their conversion.

Instead of complaining, the content of our prayer should be blessing according to Romans 12:14, *"Bless those who persecute you; bless and do not curse them"* remembering to *"repay no one evil for evil, but give thought to do what is honorable in the sight of all"* (Romans 12:17, 1 Thessalonians. 5:15), and that *"all who desire to live a godly life in Christ Jesus will be persecuted*" (1 Timothy 3:12). Therefore by gracious prayer, love abounds for God and men, simultaneously fulfilling the greatest commandments!

II. Intercessory Prayer Demonstrates Great Faith

In the Gospels, only two people are noted by Christ for their "*great faith*" as demonstrated through their prayers. In contrast, the disciples were reminded six times of their "*little faith*" (Matthew 6:30, 8:26, 14:31, 16:8, 17:20, Luke 12:28).

The first example was the political leader of Jesus' own city of ministry. So great was the Centurion's faith that Jesus marveled. His faith in the deity of Jesus and the authority of His Word led him to petition Christ with an absolute confidence that his prayer could be answered. He interceded for his servant in Matthew 8:8-9, stating that he was "*not worthy*" for Jesus to come under his roof, but needed only to speak "*the word*" and his servant would be healed. He is the first recorded believer to lead the Church in this great faith, demonstrating a greater confidence in the authority of Christ and His Word than Jesus' own touch or physical presence. While enjoying the physical presence of Christ, he led the future Church in faith, his complete confidence resting entirely on God's Word.

Jesus said of him, "*Assuredly I say to you, I have not found such great faith, not even in Israel*" (Matthew 8:10, NKJV). His faith eclipsed that of John the Baptist, the greatest prophet, Mary, the mother of Christ, and certainly all of the disciples. And it is here that Christ first introduces the Gentile Church as the future people of God: *"Many will come from the East and West* [Gentiles] *and recline at the table with Abraham, Isaac, and Jacob in the kingdom of heaven, while the sons of the kingdom will be thrown into the outer darkness. In that place there will be weeping and gnashing of teeth"* (Matthew 8:11 12). Oh that our faith were so strong in the Word of Christ that we would fully trust His authority and promises like this political leader of Christ's city of ministry!

The second example of *"great faith"* was the Canaanite woman who persistently interceded for her daughter in Matthew 15:22-28. She was seemingly shunned and even despised by Jesus when He told her *"It is not good to take the children's bread and throw it to the little dogs"* (v. 26 NKJV). Her great faith was demonstrated through her tenacious intercession, and she overcame all obstacles with the response, *"Yes, Lord; yet even the little dogs feed on the crumbs which fall from their master's table"* (v. 27 NKJV). The Lord then places her in the *"great faith"* hall of fame and grants her request (v. 28).

Both of these who interceded believed confidently with a faith that prevailed. They were not only granted what they requested, but they were also commended for their *"great faith"* by Jesus Christ. The greatness of our faith will be demonstrated by the conviction and tenacity of our prayer life, particularly as we fulfill the command of Christ in praying for "*kings and all who are in authority*" (1 Timothy 2:1-2). Even in our present political climate, when was the last time we prayed with confidence and thanksgiving for the salvation of our political leaders? What does this say of our faith?

III. Consistent Prayer was a Primary and Continual Focus of the Early Church

Following Christ's ascension, when the Church was without His physical presence for the first time, her first continuous corporate act was to meet for prayer. "*These all continued with one accord in prayer and supplication.*" (Acts 1:14 NKJV) The apostles, the women, Jesus' family and those gathered with them, comprising one hundred twenty total, were in *one accord*, their singular focus being prayer. Their unity centered in their devotion to prayer.

When the Holy Spirit came "*like a mighty rushing wind*" on the day of Pentecost, they were all in "*one accord*" (Acts 2:1 NKJV) unified in continual prayer, and suddenly they were all "*filled with the Holy Spirit*" and began to proclaim the gospel first in Jerusalem, the capital. That day three thousand were added to the Church (Acts 2:41). Even after their number had mushroomed and many needed to be taught the Word, prayer was still their first priority (Acts 2:42).

We read of the early Church: "*So continuing daily with one accord in the temple, and breaking bread from house* to house, they ate their food with gladness and generosity of heart" (Acts 2:46 NKJV) And what were they doing "*daily with one accord in the temple?*" "*Now Peter and John were going up to the temple at the hour of prayer*" (Acts 3:1). To the godly Jew throughout their history, the Temple was their "*house of prayer.*" It was this reality that caused the wrath of Christ to fall on those who would turn this "*House of Prayer*" into a "*den of thieves*" (Mt. 21:13, Mk. 11:17). The Temple was the public meeting place of the early Church for daily prayer.

When the membership of the Church surged to five thousand men (Acts 4:4), the Apostles were severely threatened (Acts 4:17), and prayer was their first response to persecution: "*So when they heard this, they lifted their voices to God with one accord*" (Acts 4:24). And, "*when they had **prayed**, the place where they had gathered together was shaken, and they were **all filled** with the Holy Spirit, and began to speak the Word of God with boldness*" (Acts 4:31). The final answer to their prayer was that "*with great power the apostles were giving testimony to the resurrection of the Lord Jesus, and abundant grace was upon them **all***" (Acts 4:33, emphasis added).

Notice again the continual mention of unity in the context of prayer. Throughout Acts, every time "*one accord*" is used in the context of the assembled Church, it is always in connection with prayer (Acts 1:14, 2:1, 2:46, 4:24, 5:12,

15:25). Since prayer was their continual focus, they also enjoyed continual unity.

IV. Prayer was a First Priority for Church Leaders

In the context, the Apostles are stretched to the limit. Five thousand men (likely with their families) in the Church, if divided equally among the twelve, would be 416 families per pastor. Thus complaining first divides the Church: the Hellenistic widows were being neglected, and these social issues required that the Apostles carefully define their pastoral priorities. After more than three years of intimate daily training with Christ, what do the all the Apostles agree is most important? *"But we will devote ourselves to prayer and to the ministry of the Word"* (Acts 6:4).

These two priorities reveal their confidence in the power of God as the foundation of their ministry. According to the Apostles, *"prayer and the ministry of the Word"* are the foundational job description for the leaders of the Church. They realize they only have two human means of power, but what more do they need? Their non-negotiable priorities declare: "IN GOD WE TRUST." Later Paul, the model and teacher regarding Church ministry (1 Cor. 15:10), also demonstrates these two essential priorities:

> *"For God, whom I serve in my spirit in the **preaching of the gospel** of His Son, is my witness as to how unceasingly I make mention of you, **always in my prayers.**"* (Romans 1:9-10 NASB, emphasis added).

24

Paul lived this priority of prayer (Philippians 1:3-4, Colossians 4:12, 1 Thessalonians 1:2, 2 Thessalonians 2:13, 2 Timothy 1:3, Philemon 1:4). His care for all the churches was primarily demonstrated through prayer for them (2 Corinthians 11:28), which he unceasingly offered in their behalf: *"For this reason, because I have heard of your faith in the Lord Jesus and your love toward all the saints,* **I do not cease to give thanks for you, remembering you in my prayers"** (Ephesians 1:15-16). *"We give thanks to God, the Father of our Lord Jesus Christ,* **praying always for you.**" (Colossians 1:3 NASB, emphasis added).

V. Prayer Engages the Power of God for Ministering the Word, Saving Leaders and Impacting Nations

Therefore what happened when the Apostles returned to the priorities of prayer and ministry of the Word? *"Then the Word of God continued to increase, and the number of the disciples multiplied greatly in Jerusalem, and a great many of the priests became obedient to the faith"* (Acts 6:7). As demonstrated in the multiplication of believers, particularly among the priests as the leaders of Israel, this kingdom strategy was peculiarly blessed of God to impact the nation through their capital ministry. (According to the commentators, if the population was about 80,000 in Jerusalem at the time of Christ, then the 5000 men and their families would represent at least 25,000 people before the multiplication of converts mentioned in this passage.)

If this multiplication represents each man winning just one other man with his family, then well over half the capital city would have been won for Christ!

According to this passage:

- The Word of God became a growing interest and conviction in the lives of the people in the capital.

- In contrast to the earlier increase of the church, there was now exponential growth. Here disciples were not simply "*added*" as earlier in Acts, but "*multiplied greatly*" through the priority and example of the church leadership in "*prayer and the ministry of the word.*"

- A "*great many*" others in leadership in the capital demonstrated a transformed life through obedience to the Scriptures.

The apostles here fulfill the commission and instruction of Christ, who also made prayer a foundation of His ministry. They no doubt remembered His words before sending them out in Matthew 9:37-38: "*The harvest is plentiful, but the laborers are few.*" We would expect at this point for Him to issue their marching orders and command them to "Go!" Instead however, His command to them focused on prayer: "*therefore **pray earnestly** to the Lord of the harvest, to send out laborers into His harvest*".

Perhaps the greatest example of this principle in action is found in dying prayer of Stephen. When he was brought before the Sanhedrin (the ruling body or Congress of Israel), Stephen ministers the Word and then prays. We see his boldness as he applies God's truth to his leaders. His prayer then becomes his Last Will and Testament as the first martyr of the Church:

> "'*You stiff-necked people, uncircumcised in heart and ears, you always resist the Holy Spirit. As your fathers did, so do you. Which of the prophets did not your fathers persecute? And they killed those who announced beforehand the coming of the Righteous One, whom you have now betrayed and murdered, you who received the law as delivered by angels and did not keep it.' Now when they heard these things they were enraged, and they ground their teeth at him. But he, full of the Holy Spirit, gazed into heaven and saw the glory of God, and Jesus standing at the right hand of God. And he said, 'Behold, I see the heavens opened and the Son of Man standing at the right hand of God.' But they cried out with a loud voice and stopped their ears and rushed together at him. Then they cast him out of the city and stoned him. And the witnesses laid down their garments at the feet of a young man named Saul. And as they were stoning Stephen, he called out, 'Lord Jesus, receive my spirit.*" (Acts 7:51-59).

Imagine being there and hearing his final prayer: "*And falling to his knees he cried out with a loud voice, 'Lord, do not hold this sin against them.' And when he had said this, he fell asleep.*" (vs.60) Stephen's final prayer models that of Christ upon the cross, (Luke 23:46, 34) and both occasions of prayer are answered through the salvation of the leaders carrying out their execution! The centurion with authority over Christ's execution believed on Him. From heaven, Jesus Christ personally answered Stephen's prayer, arresting the arrestor on the road to Damascus in Acts 9. This became another great proof of the resurrection, as the risen Lord revealed Himself to Saul and changed his heart. His direction and zeal are suddenly transformed, and God uses Saul to become the greatest evangelist (1 Cor. 15:10) and divinely-inspired author of the New Testament. What a tremendous answer to Stephen's prayer for his leaders!

VI. Prayer is Paul's "First of All" Exhortation to the Church and Pastors in Particular

It is Paul the persecutor (a title used only in 1 Timothy 1:13) who provides this foundational and final exhortation to Pastor Timothy of Ephesus, and by extension to every pastor today. Pastors, this exhortation is primarily written for your instruction and success in ministry. The Holy Spirit inspired this epistle to *"the household of God, which is the church of the living God, the pillar and buttress of the truth"* (1 Timothy 3:15). Uniquely here in Scripture we find this four-fold description of prayer as a first priority for ministry: *"Therefore I exhort first of all that supplications, prayers, intercessions, and giving of thanks, be made for all men, for kings and all who are in authority, that we may lead a quiet and peaceable life in all godliness and reverence. For this is good and acceptable in the sight of God our Savior, who desires all men to be saved, and to come to the knowledge of the truth*" (1 Timothy 2:1-4 NKJV).

Further emphasizing the priority of prayer in this epistle, we do not find another exhortation in 1 Timothy until chapter six, verse two, where pastors are commanded to "*Teach and exhort these things.*" In the intervening chapters, Paul covers all the vital basics of Church life: public and private prayer, proper roles of men and women in the Church, qualifications of pastors and deacons, authority structures in the Church and home, family relationships within the church, responsibilities to widows, responsibilities to elders, etc. Although it is most often neglected, God makes prayer a priority in this epistle over all the other essential elements that were presented to the Church leaders.

Prayer for "*all who are in authority*" is an exhortation to pray for spiritual leaders in addition to our political leaders. Paul on behalf of all pastors, often requested prayer. "*Now I beg you, brethren, through the Lord Jesus Christ and through the love of the Spirit, that you strive together with me in prayers to God for me*" (Romans 15:30 NKJV). "*I know that through your prayers and the help of the Spirit of Jesus Christ this will turn out for my deliverance*" (Philippians 1:19). 1 Thessalonians 5:25, "*Brothers, pray for us.*" 2 Thessalonians 3:1, "*Finally, brothers, pray for us that the Word of the Lord may speed ahead and be honored, as happened among you.*"

Hebrews 13:18, *"Pray for us"* (also see 1 Corinthians 1:11, Philemon 1:22). Therefore essential to Church life and ministry are public and private prayers, first and foremost for our pastors and spiritual leaders.

We expect pastors to remember their flock in prayer, but here God commissions the entire church to pray for her leaders, remembering them with thanksgiving. Pastors, are you teaching your people by example and precept the priority of prayer for leaders? Do you remember to pray especially for political and spiritual leaders, not only in the formal gathering of the church, but in your private prayers? And do we remember our leaders with thanksgiving? Men, how do you think your relationship with your employer would improve if you remembered them in prayer with thanksgiving? Wives, what would it do for your relationship with your husband if you daily thanked the Lord for him as you seek God's blessing for your home? Children, while expecting your parents to pray for you, do you gratefully remember them before your Heavenly Father?

Believer, what a joy it is to your pastor, for him to know of your grateful prayers for him and his ministry. And citizen, what a blessing it would be to your political leaders if they knew you not only prayed for wisdom in their many decisions, but also thanked the Lord for them, praying for their salvation (Proverbs 21:1). As a minister to our political leaders, I can personally testify almost in every case, to their expressions of deep appreciation for the prayers of the people they represent.

VII. Prayer is the Unceasing Privilege of Believers

This priority of prayer should also carry over into a persistence and consistency in the privilege of prayer. *"Without ceasing"* describes a duty throughout the New Testament for every believer in prayer (considering this privilege with thanksgiving):

> *"Peter therefore was kept in prison: but prayer was made **without ceasing** of the church unto God for him"* (Acts 12:5 KJV, emphasis added in all the texts below).

> *"For God is my witness, whom I serve with my spirit in the gospel of his Son, that **without ceasing** I mention you always in my prayers"* (Romans 1:9-10).

> *"For this reason, because I have heard of your faith in the Lord Jesus, and your love toward all the saints, I do **not cease** to give thanks for you, remembering you in my prayers"* (Ephesians 1:15-16).

> *"And so, from the day we heard, we have **not ceased** to pray for you, asking that you may be filled with the knowledge of his will in all wisdom and understanding."* (Colossians 1:9).

> *"We give thanks to God always for you all, making mention of you in our prayers, remembering **without ceasing** your work of faith, and labor of love, and patience of hope in our Lord Jesus Christ, in the sight of our God and Father"* (1 Thessalonians 1:2-3).

> *"For this reason we also thank God **without ceasing**, because when you received the word of God which you*

heard from us, you welcomed it not as the word of men, but as it is in truth, the word of God, which also effectually works also in you who believe." (1 Thessalonians 2:13).

*"Pray **without ceasing**. Give thanks in all circumstances, for this is the will of God in Christ Jesus for you"* (1 Thessalonians 5:17-18).

*"I thank God, whom I serve with a pure conscience, as my forefathers did, as **without ceasing** I remember you in my prayers night and day"* (1 Timothy 1:3)(NKJV).

Thus, we see in this chapter the mountain of evidence regarding the priority of prayer in the lives of God's people for salvation of leaders in the advancement of His kingdom.

Prayer is:

- The Simultaneous Fulfillment of the Two Greatest Commandments;
- The Demonstration of the Greatest Faith;
- The First and Continual Emphasis of the Early Church;
- The First Essential Necessary for Church Leaders, Engaging the Power of God in Saving Leaders and Impacting a Nation;
- The "First of All" Exhortation to the Church, and finally,
- The Unceasing Privilege of Believers.

Beloved, we must pray, both publicly in the church and privately in our homes, and especially pray for our leaders.

Endnotes

5 Albert Barns, *Notes on the NT, Explanatory and Practical; Acts,* Robert Frew, Ed., (Grand Rapids: Michigan, Baker Book House, 1980), vii.

6 This is the only passage in all of Scripture where four different kinds of prayer are given, linking it to a first priority. Ephesians 6:18 may be the next greatest emphasis in requiring the good soldier to stand in his armor with two different kinds of prayer mentioned two times (4x total) to be done *"at all times."* Both Philippians 4:6 and Colossians 4:3 follow in emphasis with three kinds of prayer mentioned.

7 W.E. Vine, Merrill F. Unger, and William White, Jr., *Vine's Complete Expository Dictionary of Old and New Testament Words* (Nashville: Tennessee, Thomas Nelson Publishers, 1996), 217.

8 Ibid.

9 Ibid.

10 Cleon L. Rogers, Jr., and Cleon L. Rogers, III, *The New Linguistic and Exegetical Key to the Greek New Testament* (Grand Rapids: Michigan, Zondervan Publishing House, 1998), 489.

11 Vine, 330.

Abraham left a legacy of prayer and ministry of the Word as a light to the nations, and many of His children left the same legacy.

Understanding Daniel's unique position of power as the sole Jewish political counselor to the emperor, who among us would have counseled Daniel to pray publicly for 30 days, risking his life in disobedience to the Law of the Medes and Persians?

GOD'S KINGDOM STRATEGY AND COMMISSION

Prayer & the Ministry of the Word:
The Church's Responsibility to Her Government

The first Wednesday of February, 2009, my wife and I were distributing the Bible study notes to the legislators in our Virginia state capital. One legislator approached saying that he had good news for us. To our amazement and joy, he told us that he had just received Christ the previous Sunday night! Excitedly I said, "Please tell me more!" But he was in a hurry to get to his caucus meeting, and told me to set up an appointment with him in his office.

Later in his office the following week, he got his wife on the phone to also help tell the story. She said that she had received Christ about a year and a half earlier, but there were many struggles in living her new life for Christ. Now she was so happy that her husband had just received Christ, and she was sure that their lives would have a whole new unity and focus. The legislator then told me that he had awoken at 1:00 AM (Sunday night/Monday morning) and had wept over his sin until 4:00 AM, so that he finally "just had to receive Jesus Christ."

In a later testimonial which I have shared with others, he states: "I wanted to thank you for all your efforts on behalf of the Lord here in the General Assembly. Your constant prayers and dutiful ministry are a blessing to us all. As you know, I recently accepted Jesus Christ as my Lord and Savior. While I clearly owe that revelation to him, I do believe that your work helped bring me to that occasion. The joy, peace and grace of the Lord now fill our house and my family is eternally grateful for your assistance. Keep up the good work!"[12]

Contemplating his testimony and appreciation for our prayers and the Bible study ministry, we realized that the prayers from thousands of believers using the Virginia Leadership Prayer Lists which had been distributed in churches throughout the state were beginning to have an effect, in addition to the thousands of Bible study notes distributed among the political leaders in the capital. It was an overwhelming delight to see the Lord answering the prayers of His people, so many who have diligently and systematically interceded for their leaders on the prayer list month after month. This was the third legislator to openly profess Christ during our ministry in the Virginia capitol.

So what are the larger implications of the salvation of our political leaders? What are God's purposes regarding their evangelization and discipleship? How should the Church (and pastors in particular) respond to political issues and problems facing our nation, particularly in light of the pressures on the Church from the government? In addition to prayer which we have seen in the previous chapter, what is the responsibility of the Church to political leaders who may oppose us and threaten our present-day right to religious liberty? What are the means God uses to provide for the open communication of the gospel? What does Scripture teach us regarding the relationship of the Church to the government? Does God give the Church a clear responsibility to governmental leaders? Are there any clear patterns throughout Scripture providing examples of believers interacting with their government officials?

These are questions we hope to address in this and succeeding chapters, focusing first on the church's primary responsibility to governmental leaders, providing examples from the Old and New Testaments, including the ministry of Christ. In the previous chapter, we laid out the church's first priority toward her political leaders: grateful prayer for them and their salvation. In this chapter, we will focus more on the second principle means found in Scripture for securing the salvation of our political leaders, which in turn provides for the widespread communication of the gospel throughout the nation.

I. The Preaching of the Prophets

Consider first how the prophets from Abraham to John the Baptist proclaimed God's truth to their leaders, seeking to turn their hearts to God. Almost without exception the prophets proclaimed the Word of God to kings.

Prophet	King or Leader	Message
1. **Abraham** (Gen. 20:7)	King of Sodom King of Salem	Gen 14:17-24

Abraham by faithful words and actions testified to the glory of God before the king of Sodom, refusing his offer of the spoils of war: *"I have lifted my hand to the LORD, God Most High, Possessor of heaven and earth, that I would not take a thread or a sandal strap or anything that is yours, lest you should say, I have made Abraham rich."[13]* **He would not let this king rob his God of any glory, also proving his motive for rescuing Lot and his household was love rather than any personal gain.**

Later, Abraham continued interceding for these same wicked cities, even when God told him of their impending destruction for violent homosexuality.[14] Abraham left a legacy of prayer and ministry of the Word as a light to the nations, and many of His children left the same legacy.

Prophet	King or Leader	Message
2. **Joseph** (Gen. 41:1-44)	Pharoah	Gen. 41
3. **Moses** (Deut. 34:10)	Pharoah	Exodus 3-14
4. **Aaron** (Ex. 7:1)	Pharoah	Exodus 3-14
5. **Samuel** (I Sam.3:20)	Saul, King of Israel	1 Sam.12:23-24

Samuel's statement to King Saul and the nation is one of the clearest passages in the Old Testament regarding the responsibility of God's people to their leaders: "*Moreover, as for me, far be it from me that I should sin against the LORD by ceasing to pray for you, and I will instruct you in the good and the right way. Only fear the LORD, and serve him faithfully with all your heart: for consider what great things He has done for you.*" (1 Samuel 12:23-24).   On Saul's coronation day, Samuel, the first prophet, addresses the first king (along with the people), providing this loving emphasis on prayer and the ministry of the Word, and reminding the king and nation of God's kind provision for them at his coronation to leadership.[15] Samuel's burden for the king and the people of God obligated him to prayer and faithful instruction in the Word, so that by word and example he confessed that the lack of prayer would be a sin against God, His king, and His people.

Here we find one of the clearest statements of Scripture which teaches us that a failure to pray is a sin against God and others.

He later demonstrated this love again through persistent intercession for his king when he received the dreaded edict of God against Saul:

> "*Then the word of the LORD came to Samuel, saying, 'I regret that I have made Saul king, for he has turned back from following Me and has not carried out My commands. And Samuel was distressed and **he cried out to the LORD all night**.*" (I Samuel 15:10-11 NASB, emphasis added)

Prophet	King or Leader	Message
6. **David** (Acts 2:30)	King Saul	1 Samuel 26:19-21
7. **Gad** (I Samuel 22:5)	King David	I Samuel 22
8. **Nathan** (II Sam.7:2)	King David	II Sam.7, 12; I Kgs 1
9. **Ahijah** (I Kgs 11:29)	Jeroboam (Israel)	I Kings 11:26-40
10. **Jehu** (I Kings 16:7)	Baasha (Israel)	I Kings 16:1-7
11. **Elijah** (I Kings 18:36)	Ahab (Israel)	I Kings 17-19
	Hazael (Syria)	I Kings 19:15
	Jehu (Israel)	I Kings 19:15
12. **Obadiah** (Obadiah 1)	Ahab (Israel)	I Kings 18:3-16
13. **Micaiah** (I Kings 22:8)	Ahab (Israel)	I Kings 22:1-39
	Jehoshaphat (Judah)	
14. **Elisha** (I Kings 19:16)	Jehoram (Israel)	2 Kings 3
	Jehoshaphat (Judah)	2 Kings 3
	The King of Edom	2 Kings 3
	Naaman-Syrian army head	2 Kings 5
	Ben-Hadad-King of Syria	2 Kings 6-7
	Hazael-King of Syria	2 Kings 8:7-15
	Jehu-grandson of Nimshi	2 Kings 9:1-13
	Joash (Israel)	2 Kings 13:14-25
15. **Joel** (Joel 1:1)	Elders of Israel	Joel 1:2
16. **Jonah** (2 Kings 14:25)	Amaziah (Judah)	2 Kings 14:23-27
	Jeroboam (Israel)	2 Kings 14:23-27
	King of Nineveh	Jonah 3:6

Elijah and Elisha do not leave their country, Israel, though they minister to foreign leaders (see above). But Jonah is commissioned to go to the indescribably cruel people of the capital of the Assyrian empire.

The deep sorrow and rigorous repentance of Nineveh through the preaching of Jonah may have been the greatest revival in Bible history, resulting in the salvation of at least 600,000 repentant Ninevites, more than the 3000 and 5000 converted at the time of Pentecost. The commentator Hugh Martin tells us:

> "The repentance of Nineveh is one of the most singular events in history. A great and proud city suddenly smitten into the most profound humiliation, from the greatest of its inhabitants unto the least of them, -from the king on the throne to the meanest citizen - is a spectacle to which, I suppose, history affords no parallel. Cities, and countries, and communities have oftentimes, with not a little unanimity, given themselves to humiliation and fasting. But there is no event on record that can at all be compared with the fast and repentance of Nineveh." [16]

This revival was led by a Gentile king and his nobles.[17] Note the Scripture text:

> "*And the people of Nineveh believed God. They called for a fast, and put on sackcloth, **from the greatest to the least of them**. The word [had] reached the **king of Nineveh**, and he arose from his throne, removed his robe, covered himself with sackcloth, and sat in ashes. And he issued*

*a proclamation and published through Nineveh, 'By the decree of the **king and his nobles**: Let neither man nor beast, herd nor flock, taste anything. Let them not feed or drink water, But let man and beast be covered with sackcloth, and let them call out mightily to God. Let everyone turn from his evil way and from the violence that is in his hands. Who knows? God may turn and relent, and turn from His fierce anger, so that we may not perish.'"* (Jonah 3:5-9).

In Jonah's dreadful words, *"Still forty days and Nineveh shall be overthrown!"*, which brought repentance in the hearts of these political leaders, we see six reasons for their hope:

1) Historically, the Assyrian armies from Nineveh would usually surround a city, warn it of its impending doom and give the city an opportunity to surrender before destroying it. They probably would have seen the parallel in Jonah's proclamation.

2) The fact that they were given warning meant that they had an opportunity to repent.

3) The reality that they were provided 40 days would give them sufficient time to demonstrate their repentance.

4) If the king and his people followed the decree *"not to feed or drink water"* for 40 days, then they would have to be miraculously sustained by God in their repentance.

5) The meaning of the word *"overthrown"* also included the concept of "turned" so this phrase could be understood as a declaration of their turning within the 40 days.

6) Jonah's own disobedience, repentance, and miraculous deliverance was a "*sign*" to the Ninevites (Luke 11:30). Jonah probably didn't like retelling his story, but his appearance after being vomited from the belly of the great fish must have excited their curiosity and required an explanation.

But the most exciting point of this narrative is that the leaders' repentance becomes the example and pattern of repentance for the entire capital city of the Assyrian empire. E.P. Alldredge, in his commentary on Jonah, captures the capital strategy in reaching Nineveh – which God twice calls "*that great city*" at the beginning and end of the book (1:2, 4:11):

> "The fate of the greatest nations also has from the beginning been bound up with *great cities*... The spread of Christianity, in the beginning and its progress today, was and is and will continue to be bound up with the *great cities*. So that, as go the *great cities* of our day, so will go the fate of our nation and our civilization—and to a very large degree the progress of God's kingdom."[18] (emphasis added)

The humble repentance of this king and his nobles not only led the men of Nineveh to repent, but provided a bold witness to the surrounding nations, since Nineveh was the capital of the largest empire of that day. Their repentance would have been a beacon to the world at that time.

Prophet	King or Leader	Message
17. **Amos** (Amos 1:1)	Uzziah (Judah)	Amos 1:2
	Jereboam (Israel)	Amos 1:2, 7:10-13
18. **Hosea** (Hosea 1:1)	Jeroboam (Israel)	Hosea 1:1, 5:1
	Uzziah (Judah)	Hosea 1:1
	Jotham (Judah)	Hosea 1:1
	Ahaz (Judah)	Hosea 1:1
	Hezekiah (Judah)	Hosea 1:1

19. **Isaiah** (2 Kings 19:2) Hezekiah (Judah)   2 Kings 19:1-7
Isaiah foresaw and prophesied the salvation of the nations and their leaders:

*"**Kings** shall see and arise; princes, and they shall prostrate themselves, because of the LORD, who is faithful, and the Holy One of Israel, who has chosen You."* (Isa.49:7)

*"And nations shall come to your light and **kings** to the brightness of your rising."* (Isa. 60:3)

*"The nations shall see your righteousness, and **all the kings** your glory, and you shall be called by a new name, that the mouth of the LORD will give."* (Isa.62:2)

Prophet	King or Leader	Message
20. **Micah** (Jer.26:18)	Hezekiah (Judah)	Jeremiah 26:18-19
21. **Nahum** (Nahum 1:1)	King of Assyria	Nahum 3:18
22. **Zephaniah** (Zeph. 1:1)	Josiah (Judah)	Zephaniah
	Princes, Prophets &	Zephaniah 3:3-4
	Priests of Jerusalem	

Prophet	King or Leader	Message
23. **Jeremiah** (Jer. 25:3)	Josiah (Judah)	Jeremiah 1:2-3
	Jehoiakim (Judah)	Jeremiah 22:18
	Zedekiah (Judah)	Jeremiah 21-22
	Nebuchadnezzar-Babylon	Jeremiah 29
24. **Ezekiel** (Ez. 1:3)	Nebuchadnezzar-Babylon	Ezequiel 21-32
25. **Daniel** (Matt.24:15)	Nebuchadnezzar	Daniel 2:24-48
	Belshazzar-King of Babylon	Daniel 5:2-30
	Darius-King of the Medes	Daniel 5:30-6:28
	Cyrus-King of the Persians	Daniel 6:28

God seems to have used the faithful prayers and ministry of Daniel and the three Hebrew children to draw the prideful and wicked king, Nebuchadnezzar, to Himself. The king's witness to the nations as the leader of the first world empire (according to Daniel's vision) is evidenced in Daniel 4, an entire chapter devoted to Nebuchadnezzar's decree that *"all peoples, nations, and languages that dwell in all the earth"* be shown the majesty of *"the Most High God."*[19]

Understanding Daniel's unique position of power as the sole Jewish political counselor to the emperor, who among us would have counseled Daniel to pray publicly for 30 days, risking his life in disobedience to the Law of the Medes and Persians? (Daniel 6:7)

Daniel's faithful witness and testimony through prayer must have been used by God to win Darius, the emperor, who required *"all the peoples, nations and languages that dwell in all the earth"* to *"fear and tremble before the God of Daniel, for He is the living God, enduring forever; His kingdom shall never be destroyed, and His dominion shall be to the end."* (Dan. 6:25-28). God so richly blessed the prayers and witness of Daniel that emperors were transformed and boldly required the citizens of the world empire to *"fear"* the God of Heaven. Here is the source of peace and true freedom of religion to disciple all the nations!

The emperors Darius and Artaxerxes also commanded to uphold the decree of Cyrus who pronounced a curse upon anyone who might hinder the rebuilding of the temple in Jerusalem, and commanded to pay for the temple's construction out of the *"royal revenue"* (Ezra 6:8-14). These emperors, sometimes called *"king of kings,"*[20] valued the prayers of God's people to the degree that their stated motive in issuing this decree to rebuild the temple was to receive their prayers: *"That they may offer pleasing sacrifices to the God of heaven and **pray for the life of the king, and of his sons**."*[21]

What a tremendous impact the statesman, Daniel, and his practice of prayer must have made upon his emperors!

Prophet	King or Leader	Message
26. **Haggai** (Ezra 5:1)	Zerubbabel-Governor	Haggai 1:1
	Joshua the High Priest	Haggai 1:1
27. **Zachariah** (Zach. 1:1)	Joshua the High Priest	Zach. 3:1
28. **Malachi** (Malachi 1:1)	Priests of Israel	Mal. 2:1

Not only does this clear pattern of ministering to leaders run throughout the entire Old Testament, it also begins the New Testament, and continues to gain even clearer focus in the Greatest Prophet, Jesus Christ, the Messiah of Israel.

Prophet	King or Leader	Message

29. **John the Baptist** (Mt.11:9-15) Herod Antipas Mk.6:17-28

II. The Ministry of the Messiah

Christ's Ministry in Capernaum

The ministry of the man, Jesus Christ, was deliberate in regard to winning leaders. Jesus wins the political, business, and religious leadership of His own city of ministry, Capernaum.

1. Capernaum's political leadership

Here Jesus won both a Jewish political leader – the nobleman (John 4:46-53) and the Gentile political leader, the Centurion. The Centurion, who had built the synagogue for the city and exercised Roman authority over the city, became a believer demonstrating greater faith than anyone in all of Israel (Matthew 8:5-13, Luke 7:1-10).

We saw the Centurion's spiritual leadership earlier as he entered the "*great faith*" hall of fame. Although this political leader of Capernaum receives the accolades of Jesus, he is not alone in his humility and faith in Christ.

2. Capernaum's business leadership

Matthew the publican, is a business leader sitting at the gate collecting taxes in this major city of Galilee, the northern tax center for Rome. Jesus commands this notoriously corrupt businessman, *"Follow Me"*, and the response was an immediate and unquestioning obedience: *"he arose and followed Him"* (Matthew 9:9). Matthew leads all the authors of the New Testament, according to the unanimous witness of the early Church fathers, in writing the first gospel.[22]

3. Capernaum's spiritual leadership

The humility and faith in Christ demonstrated by Jairus, the ruler of the synagogue in Capernaum is also dramatic. According to the accounts of the synoptic Gospels, it is clear that while Matthew was having a dinner for Jesus at his house, the Pharisees arrogantly asked His disciples, *"Why does your Teacher eat with tax collectors and sinners?"* (Mt. 9:11) *"While He was saying these things to them, behold, a ruler came in and knelt before Him, saying, 'My daughter has just died, but come and lay your hand on her and she will live'"* (Mt. 9:18). So Jairus, the ruler of the Synagogue, *"falling at Jesus' feet, implored Him to come to his house"* (Luke 8:41). Boldly ignoring the scorn of his colleagues and possible smirks of the publicans, he humbly threw himself at Jesus' feet, suddenly bringing a hush to the banquet with his plea from a believing heart. Jesus responded with His second resurrection from the dead for His own synagogue ruler.

Christ's Strategic Commission

All the Synoptic Gospels present the commission of Christ to His disciples to testify of Him before governors and kings (cf. Mt. 10:18, Mk. 13:9, Lk. 21:12). *"You will be brought before kings and governors for My name's sake"* indicating yet again His Kingdom strategy and the boldness provided for witnessing, even in time of persecution.

Christ's ministry in the capital city of Jerusalem

As the religious and political center of Israel which would later suffer divine judgment and national destruction due to the rejection of their Messiah, Jesus wept over His own capital of Jerusalem (Lk.19:41). Approaching His impending trial and execution in that city, the raising of Lazarus from the dead near Jerusalem later resulted in many Jews believing on Him (Jn.11:45), as well as many of the rulers (Jn.12:42). Even at His death, the Centurion responsible for His execution believed (Mt. 27:54). Two wealthy leaders of the Sanhedrin described as disciples in John 19:38-39 buried Him: Joseph of Arimathea, and Nicodemus, the teacher of Israel (Jn. 3:10). Christ's profound and powerful presentation of the gospel was recorded for that spiritual leader (John 3). Jesus' last and boldest confession of Gospel truth was made to the king over His capital, Pontius Pilate (1 Tim. 6:13). Just as in Capernaum, Jesus witnessed to both His religious and political leaders in Jerusalem, the capital.

Jesus not only leads by His example in prayer and the ministry of the Word to his leaders, but in His commissions He strategically passes on His mission to the Church.

III. The Clarity of the Commissions

As outlined in the introduction, the commissions align in a crescendo of emphasis on leaders. In the imperative of the Great Commission to "*disciple all the nations*" Jesus presents "*the nations*" as people groups to disciple rather than just individuals among the nations. John Piper, at the end of his extensive study in Matthew 28:19-20 says, "Therefore in all likelihood Jesus did not send His apostles out with a general mission merely to win as many individuals as they could, but rather to reach all the peoples of the world."[23] Since Christ's command is to disciple nations, then the Great Commission requires a strategy which would have to include leaders and would even include an emphasis on where the gospel was to be presented.

Christ's emphasis on Jerusalem, the first capital of Christianity

The commission in Christ's final words to the early Church before His ascension emphasizes capitals. Jesus commanded that evangelism begin, not in His own center of ministry (Capernaum) nor His hometown (Nazareth) nor even the place of His birth (Bethlehem), but "*that repentance and forgiveness of sins should be proclaimed in His name to all the nations, beginning from Jerusalem"* (Lk. 24:47). They were required to *"tarry in the city of Jerusalem"* (Lk. 24:49 NKJV), and were *"not to depart from Jerusalem but to wait for the promise of the Father"* (Acts 1:4). Including Acts 1:8, there are four separate occasions where Christ required His disciples to begin in Jerusalem. If we include the later occasions where Jerusalem is mentioned in their immediate obedience to Christ's words, the capital of Jerusalem is mentioned seven times.

Prophecy's emphasis on Jerusalem

This witness of the gospel going forth from the religious capital of the world had been prophesied hundreds of years earlier as the city *"in the latter days,"* into which *"all the nations shall flow"*. ...*"For out of Zion shall go the Law, and the word of the Lord from Jerusalem"* (Isaiah 2:2-3).

The prophecy that Peter quotes as fulfilled on the day of Pentecost also requires that their witness begin in the capital:

"And it shall come to pass afterward that I will pour out My Spirit on all flesh; your sons and your daughters shall prophesy, your old men shall dream dreams, and your young men shall see visions. And also on My menservants and on My maidservants I will pour out My Spirit in those days. And I will show wonders in the heavens and in the earth: Blood and fire and pillars of smoke. The sun shall be turned into darkness, and the moon into blood, before the coming of the great and awesome day of the

LORD. And it shall come to pass that whoever calls on the name of the LORD shall be saved. For in Mount Zion and in Jerusalem there shall be deliverance, as the LORD has said, among the remnant whom the LORD calls." (Joel 2:28-32 NKJV)

Thus both prophecy and Christ demanded that the gospel begin in the capital of Israel, and it would then move onward and upward to Rome, the capital of the world empire.

Christ's Kingdom Commission for the strategic capitals of the nations

Consider the emphasis in Acts 1:8. *"But you will receive power when the Holy Spirit has come upon you; and you shall be My witnesses in Jerusalem, and in all Judea, and Samaria, and to the end of the earth."* From *"Jerusalem,"* the capital of Israel, they were to go into the region where most of the leaders of Israel lived – *"Judea"*, and then to the next closest capital – *"Samaria,"* and then *"to the end of the earth."*

"The end of the earth" (εσχατου της γης) had a significant meaning in the way it is used in the Septuagint (LXX – the Greek translation of the Hebrew Old Testament Scriptures) with which Christ and His Apostles were familiar. This exact phrase is used 13 times in the LXX, and speaks of superiority, extremity, and finality.[24] In Isaiah 49:6-7 *"the end of the earth"* climaxes with reference to kings. The first use in Deuteronomy 28:48-49 references an empire *"from the end of the earth"* as an *"eagle"* subduing Israel with a *"yoke of iron"*. In Isaiah 8:7-9 the phrase speaks

52

of the Assyrian Empire from Nineveh. Isaiah 48:20 and Jeremiah 6:22, 25:32, 50:41 all reference the world empire of Babylon with this phrase. Therefore, this phrase "*the end of the earth*" seems to have much more to do with national superiority and greatness than actual distance. So the Apostles from their own translation of the Old Testament Scriptures, could have logically understood this phrase to refer to Rome, the capital of the current world empire.

John Polhill in his commentary on Acts 1:8 gives another evidence from Scripture to consider this phrase as referring to Rome: "'The *'end of the earth'* is often taken as referring to Rome, since the story of Acts ends in that city."[25] A. T. Robertson says of Acts 1:8, "'The Acts themselves form the best commentary on these words, and the words themselves might be given as the best summary of Acts' [Robertson quoting Page]. The events follow this outline: Jerusalem till the end of chapter 7, with the martyrdom of Stephen, the scattering of the saints through Judea and Samaria in chapter 8, the conversion of Saul, chapter 9, the spread of the gospel to Romans in Caesarea by Peter (Chapter 10), to Greeks in Antioch (Chapter 11), finally Paul's world tours and arrest and arrival in Rome (chapters 11 to 28)."[26] Other commentators, Richard Rackham,[27] and Stan Toussaint[28] also agree that the final phrase of Acts 1:8, '*the end of the earth*' refers to Rome. William Barclay underscores the same thesis when he says:

"This plan of Acts explains the very fact about Acts which at first sight is most puzzling. Why does Acts finish where it does? It finishes with Paul in prison awaiting judgment. We would so much have liked to know what happened to Paul, but the end is wrapped in mystery. But Luke stopped there because his purpose was accomplished. He has shown how Christianity began in Jerusalem and swept across the world until it reached the great city of Rome. A great New Testament scholar has said that the title of Acts might be, 'How they brought the Good News from Jerusalem to Rome.' Luke's aim was to set before men the well-nigh miraculous spread of the gospel, and he laid down his pen when he had shown Christianity established in the capital of the world."[29]

William Taylor speaking of Rome as Paul's final destination in fulfillment of Acts 1:8, states: "The beloved physician Luke has carried his history no farther, his design evidently being to bring up his narrative to that point at which, in the person of its chiefest apostle, the power of God in the gospel was brought into contact with the power of the world in its strongest seat."[30]

Howard Marshall focuses even more clearly on this end when he states regarding the book of Acts, "In a broad sense it can be said that the purpose of the account is to show how the gospel, in the person of Paul, came to Rome."[31] So, the book of Acts, written by Luke the medical doctor to the Governor, Theophilus, begins and ends with this emphasis on reaching leaders in capitals.

Is it best to interpret Acts 1:8 only in terms of geographical expansion?

Many have understood the commission of Acts 1:8 to refer simply to the geographical expansion of the gospel, beginning at Jerusalem, the location of the early NT church, and branching out from there. While not denying that this indeed occurred in the book of Acts, this limited view needs to be expanded since it fails to account for a number of facts here presented:

1) It fails to recognize the cities of Acts 1:8 as capitals.
2) It overlooks the repeated pattern in the Old and New Testaments of ministry to kings and those in authority.
3) It fails to unify the commissions in a coherent plan, or provide for an overall strategy in the discipling of the nations.
4) It fails to understand the New Testament commissions as outlining God's strategy in the fulfillment of His command to disciple the nations.
5) It fails to recognize the strategic nature of Paul's commission in Acts 9:15, fulfilling Acts 1:8 and his strategic ministry in capitals, especially culminating in Rome the imperial capital.
6) It fails to recognize the development of the commissions found initially in the Old Testament and continued in the New, beginning in seed form in Matthew 28:19-20, and finding its full and final directive in 1 Timothy 2:1-4, which centers on the salvation of leaders with resounding emphasis.

However, if the NT commissions present a unified strategy as outlined in this book, then we would expect those evangelists modeled in the book of Acts to follow this geopolitical interpretation of Acts 1:8 – a geographical expansion emphasizing the evangelization of political leaders in the capital cities. This is precisely what we find throughout the book of Acts and the resultant history of the New Testament church. In addition to Stephen's witness to the Sanhedrin, the ruling body of Israel, three people in the book of Acts lived to demonstrate this geopolitical model: Peter, Philip, and Paul.

Peter's Fulfillment of the Kingdom Commission

Peter, with all the Apostles, obediently begins evangelizing the capital city of **Jerusalem** (Acts 1:12-8:1) and 3000 are saved. The Church then mushrooms to 5000 men, and "*many of the priests became obedient to the faith*" as we saw earlier. Saul, through persecution, drives the Church to scatter "*throughout **the regions** of Judea and Samaria*" (Acts 8:1), and "*those who were scattered went about preaching the word*" (Acts 8:4).

The next intentional thrust of evangelism is in the next closest capital, **Samaria**. "*Philip went down to the **city** of Samaria and proclaimed to them the Christ. And the crowds with one accord paid attention to what was being said by Philip*" (Acts 8:5-6). When the Apostles heard "*that Samaria received the word of God*" (Acts 8:14), Peter and John went and "*prayed for them*" (Acts 8:15) and "*laid their hands on them, and they received the Holy Spirit*" (Acts 8:17).

This does not mean that other regions were to be neglected. The Kingdom Commission model to capitals does not exclude the other regions. Note what Peter and John did on the way home: "*When they had testified and spoken the word of the Lord, they returned to Jerusalem, preaching the gospel in many villages of the Samaritans*" (Acts 8:25). They evangelized as they could in the rural areas as they traveled back to Jerusalem.

In Acts 9:32, Peter is again in focus as he ministers to the saints in Lydda, the seat of the Sanhedrin when meeting with the Romans.[32] Upon healing Aeneas, "*all the residents of Lydda and Sharon saw him and they turned to the Lord*" (Acts 9:35). "*Since Lydda was near Joppa, the disciples, hearing that Peter was there, sent two men to him, urging him, 'Please come to us without delay'*" (Acts 9:38). There Peter heals Dorcas, "*And it became known throughout all Joppa, and many believed in the Lord. And he stayed in Joppa for many days with one Simon, a tanner*" (Acts 9:42-43).

From Joppa, Peter's evangelism is supernaturally and strategically directed in Acts 10 to Caesarea, the Roman capital over Judea,[33] and there he wins a military leader, Cornelius, to faith in Christ. This man was a centurion of the Italian regiment (probably from Rome) who was both a Roman leader and "*well-spoken of by the whole Jewish nation*" (Acts 10:22). The leadership of the centurion is evident as he believes with all "*his relatives and close friends*" (Acts 10:24, 44).

Following Herod's attempt to kill Peter in Jerusalem, he flees and stays for some time in Caesarea (Acts 12:19), the Roman capital where Herod lives. Much later at the occasion when Peter is rebuked by Paul, he was in Antioch, the capital of Syria (Galatians 2:11). History tells us he was martyred in Rome, *the end of the earth.*

Philip's Fulfillment of the Kingdom Commission

Like Peter, Philip's evangelism is also supernaturally directed. *"Now an angel of the Lord said to Philip, 'Rise and go toward the south to the road that goes down from Jerusalem to Gaza.' This is a desert place"* (Acts 8:26). Some may be quick to question here whether the Kingdom Commission model breaks down, since there was no capital in the desert. However, the passage goes on to state, *"So he arose and went. And behold, a man of Ethiopia, a eunuch of great authority under Candice the queen of the Ethiopians, who had charge of all her treasury and had come to Jerusalem to worship, was returning. And sitting in his chariot, he was reading Isaiah the prophet. Then the Spirit said to Philip, 'Go near and overtake the chariot'"* (Acts 8:27-29 NKJV).

Philip wins the eunuch to Christ from Isaiah 53 and baptizes him (Acts 8:30-38) as a convert of the early Jerusalem church. Like Joseph to Pharaoh, this eunuch serves Candice the queen of the Ethiopians, thus providing the gospel through him to the capital of Ethiopia, and according to history, founding a church there.[34]

For Philip in this case, to win a leader was to plant a church and influence or possibly even disciple a nation.

Following the example of Peter and John on their way back from Samaria, Philip the Evangelist "*as he passed through, he kept preaching the gospel to all the cities until he came to Caesarea*" (Acts 8:40 NASB). Philip seems to have remained in Caesarea, the Roman capital over Judea, because he is still residing there about twenty years later (Acts 21:8). Apparently, Philip settled in Caesarea and spent most of his life there, probably seeking to win to Christ the leadership among the Romans occupying his own country. The inclusion of Philip and Stephen in the same strategic evangelism as the Apostles demonstrates that the commissions were understood to include all disciples in general.

Paul's Fulfillment of the Kingdom Commission

There was one particular leader residing in Jerusalem with superior giftedness, leadership and zeal above the other Jewish leaders, yet initially the greatest enemy of the Church. He had presided over the stoning of Stephen (Acts 7:58), and consented to his death (Acts 8:1). Religiously, he was a powerful man in the world of his day. He had the legal power to go into a foreign country, arrest citizens of that country, and bring them back into his own country to try them and execute them (Acts 9:1-2). However, in response to Stephen's witness to the Sanhedrin and his dying prayer for them answered by Christ's direct revelation from heaven to Saul, this leader was converted in partial fulfillment of Christ's Kingdom Commission (Acts 9:3-9).

The King of Kings then commissioned Saul through Ananias saying, "*He is a chosen instrument of Mine, to carry My name before the Gentiles and kings and the children of Israel*" (Acts 9:15). Gentiles and Jews include all men, but in addition, he was specifically commissioned to evangelize government leaders, or kings. Therefore, since capital cities would be the only place Saul could find all three groups of people, then we might expect Saul's ministry to be in capitals.

Saul's ministry begins in **Damascus, a provincial capital of Syria,** but soon returns to **Jerusalem, the national capital of Israel.** Then he ministers in **Tarsus, the capital of Cilicia** in Asia Minor.[35] Later, Barnabas went to Tarsus and brought Saul to minister in the church at **Antioch, the capital of Syria,**[36] the third largest city in the Roman Empire.[37]

It is at Antioch that they are first called "*Christians*" (Acts 11:26), and it was from Antioch that God sent out His first mission team comprised of two elders/pastors of the church, Barnabas and Saul, and John Mark as their assistant, (the writer of the Gospel of Mark and the cousin of Barnabas) (Col.4:10; Acts 13:5).

The Capital Cities
of Paul's Missionary Journeys

We will now study in detail Paul's fulfillment of Christ's Kingdom Commission during his missionary journeys. Saul and Barnabas begin in Salamis and each city will be reviewed in sequence and studied according to its geographical / political significance.

Paul's First Missionary Journey

§ **Salamis, the largest city of Cypress**.[38] (Acts 13:4-5) Barnabas is the leader of the mission team as indicated by the order of the names, and this is Barnabas' hometown, the first city they seek to evangelize (Acts 4:36). From there they move on to the capital of the island.

🏛 **Paphos, the Capital of Cypress**.[39] (Acts 13:6-12)

Several strategic events occur in rapid succession in Paphos:

1) They "*find*" a certain Jewish magician, a false prophet named Bar-Jesus who was with the Proconsul, the King over the Isle, Sergius Paulos, an intelligent man who held the authority over the Island of Cyprus.

2) Sergius Paulos called for Barnabas and Saul and sought to hear the Word of God.

3) The magician opposed them, seeking to turn the Proconsul away from the faith and is rebuked by Saul, and struck with temporary blindness (just as Saul at his conversion).

4) The Proconsul, or **king over the island, is astonished and believes**.

5) Saul takes a **permanent name change** and is never again referred to as **"Saul," but only as "Paul."** The new name is the same **"Paulos"** by which the Proconsul is known, according to Scripture and archeology.[40]

   Apparently, this is a momentous occasion in the life of Saul and the mission team. Obeying his commission, he had won both Jews and Gentiles, and now he wins his first king. **So Saul takes the name of Paul, the first king he wins to Christ, and carries it with him the rest of his life and ministry.** Cyprian, a church father at Carthage around 250AD states clearly that "St. Paul borrowed his Roman name from Sergius Paulos,"[41] and Jerome agrees.[42]

6) Later, the order of the presentation of the names changes, indicating a **leadership change in the mission team**. Previously "Barnabas and Saul," became afterward "Paul and Barnabas."

🏛 **Perga. The Capital of Pamphylia.**[43] We are not told what happened here except that John Mark deserted the mission team from Perga (Acts 13:13). Possibly harsh words may have been spoken in this city as John Mark expressed his resentment and rejection of the new leadership of Paul in the place of his cousin, Barnabas.

🏛 **Pisidia Antioch. The Capital of Southern Galatia.**[44] Paul preaches his first biblically recorded sermon here in the synagogue and many Jews and devout proselytes believe (Acts 13:43). Then the whole city came to hear the gospel (Acts 13:44). When the envious Jews oppose Paul and Barnabas, they turn to the Gentiles publicly for the first time, and "*as many as were appointed to eternal life believed*" (Acts 13:46-48). "*But the Jews incited the devout women of high standing and the leading men of the city, and stirred up persecution against Paul and Barnabas and drove them out of their district*" (Acts 13:50).

🏛 **Iconium. The Capital of Lyconia.**[45] This city lies on the main trade route between Syrian Antioch and Ephesus. When they spoke in the synagogue, a great number of Jews and Greeks believed. But the unbelieving Jews sought to falsely accuse the believers before the unbelievers, so that Paul and Barnabas chose to stay there for a long time teaching and working miracles. This divided the city and the unbelieving Jews and Gentiles attempted to abuse and stone them. When Paul and Barnabas were made aware of it, they "*fled to Lystra and Derbe*" (Acts 14:1-6).

§ **Lystra, not a capital, a city at the foot of Black Mountain**[46]
As the first deviation from his usual fulfillment of the Kingdom Commission, we are told in Acts 14:5-6 that in Iconium "*a violent attempt was made by both the Gentiles and Jews with their rulers to abuse and stone them, they became aware of it and **fled** to Lystra and Derbe*". Luke, the inspired writer, provides a specific motive for Paul's departure from his original strategy.

However, the town of Lystra being full of rough mountain folk, was not a safe place for the missionaries, and not belonging to the pro-consular service of Rome it offered no protection by the imperial government.[47] When a cripple from birth is healed by Paul, they try to worship Barnabas as Zeus and Paul as Hermes. He had scarcely stopped their worship when Jews from Antioch and Iconium arrived and persuaded them to stone Paul. Likely, Timothy witnessed the horrible spectacle (2 Tim. 3:2) as they stoned him, dragged him outside the city and left him for dead. When the disciples gathered around Paul and prayed, he revived and returned to the city (Acts 14:8-20).

§ **Derbe, not a capital, near a Roman customs checkpoint.** As noted above, this is not a capital city, yet it became an intended refuge for Paul and his entourage during time of intense persecution (Acts 14:6). Following their persecution in these dangerous cities, they circled back through the churches of Lystra, Iconium and Antioch of Pisidia *"encouraging them to continue in the faith, and saying, that through many tribulations we must enter the kingdom of God"* (Acts 14:22). They also appointed elders in all the churches (Acts 14:23) and then returned to their sending church in Antioch, the Syrian capital.

After reporting to their sending church, they went to Jerusalem, attended the Jerusalem Council, and returned with Silas to Antioch. Peter comes to Antioch and is rebuked by Paul for shunning the Gentiles. When Paul is ready to depart again for his second missionary journey, Barnabas is unwilling to go without his cousin, John Mark. Sadly, the contention was so sharp that it divided closest friends and most effective missionary companions (Acts 14:26-15:39).

Paul's Second Missionary Journey

Barnabas and John Mark sail for Cyprus. Paul chooses Silas as his companion, and *"having been commended by the brothers to the grace of the Lord,"* they depart and go through Syria and Cilicia, strengthening the churches (Acts 15:40-41). When they arrive back at Derbe and Lystra, they find Timothy and he joins the mission team (Acts 16:1-5).

Another divine intervention gives clear direction to Paul's Kingdom Commission: *"And they went through the region of Phrygia and Galatia, having been forbidden by the Holy Spirit to speak the word in Asia. And when they had come up to Mysia, they attempted to go into Bithynia, but the Spirit of Jesus did not allow them. So, passing by Mysia, they went down to Troas. And a vision appeared to Paul in the night: a man of Macedonia was standing there, urging him and saying, 'Come over to Macedonia and help us'"* (Acts 16:6-9). In his fervent love for all men, Paul desired to go into Asia and Bithynia (away from Rome), but instead was supernaturally directed to Macedonia (Acts 16:10). The other regions he considered would have taken him farther away from a path to the *"end of the earth,"* the seat of the world empire. It seemed that the Holy Spirit was always directing him onward and upward toward Rome.

☟ **Philippi, a former capital,**[48] *"the foremost city of that part of Macedonia"* (Acts 16:12 NKJV). This is the only city of Paul's journeys where the Scriptures emphasize the significance of the city, providing the one exception that proves the rule of Christ's Kingdom Commission, through the direction of the Holy Spirit. Though formerly a capital, it is not currently a capital when Paul arrives, but the inspired writer continues to reveal the strategy of Paul. G. Campbell Morgan says of this city that "they reproduced Rome in miniature".[49] It was a greatly favored city because the men of Philippi had helped win the deciding victory in a nearby battle for Anthony and Octavius (the reigning emperor, known as Augustus), defeating Brutus and Cassius who had tried to overthrow the leadership of the Roman Empire, assassinating Julius Caesar. As an extension of Rome and formerly a capital, Philippi was the retirement city of Roman generals, which even had the right to elect its own magistrates.

Having assisted the emperor, they were especially favored through exemption from taxation, and enjoyed all the rights of Roman Citizenship as well as the privilege of direct appeal by their own magistrates to the emperor himself.[50] The lack of a synagogue here revealed the scarcity of resident Jews. It is significant that Paul chooses this city without a synagogue, demonstrating that his pattern of ministry to cities was not determined by the existence of a synagogue. Nevertheless, those who were Jews or devout Gentiles, resorted to a stream outside the city to meet. Lydia, a seller of purple in the city of Thyatira, is converted here at the preaching of Paul.

Also of significance is that here for the first time Christianity is challenged politically, and accused of opposition to the Roman government and of violating Roman law. Paul is arrested and beaten, and makes his defense based on his native-born Roman citizenship, and that his religion had never been in conflict with Roman law. He was very concerned throughout his missionary journeys to protect his reputation, so as not to lose credibility for his message of the gospel. Therefore, when Paul left Philippi as a free man, he insisted on a public exoneration. This was not a defense of his personal or political rights as a Roman citizen but rather a defense of the credibility of Christianity and the gospel. (See 1 Cor.9:19-23)[51] The Biblical means providing for the open communication of the gospel are not primarily political but spiritual, which will be discussed in chapters three and four. Paul will continue this path throughout his missionary journeys until he gives his defense of the gospel before Caesar.

The large cities of **Amphipolis** and **Apollonia** are located strategically on the Egnatian Road linking Philippi and Thessalonica, but are bypassed by the mission team. Amphipolis was even larger than Philippi.[52]

🏛 **Thessalonica. The Capital of Macedonia.**[53] Known as a strategic city for additional reasons:

1) Its nearby hot springs for which it was first called "Therma,"

2) As a free city, it enjoyed all the same privileges as Philippi, having fought on the side of the emperor in the same battle against Brutus and Cassius,

3) Geographically located where the traffic of the sea met the traffic of the land and the Egnatian Road, which connected Rome with the West, met the sea at this great city.

4) Two rivers, the Vardar and Vistritza provided transportation conduits for agricultural products from the fertile region above the city.

5) As one of the major seaports of the day, it ranked with Ephesus and Corinth in its port traffic.

6) The city formed a natural amphitheatre as it sloped gently down toward the sea.

7) It had a modern Roman network of fresh water supply and drainage system.

8) A large percentage of the population was Jewish .[54]

9) As the capital city, it was also the largest city of Macedonia.[55]

Next to Jerusalem, this city enjoyed the greatest revival of Paul's evangelistic endeavors demonstrated in the transforming zeal and the extent of the believers' response to the proclamation of the gospel. Before intense persecution erupted, Paul had only three weeks to preach the gospel, going to the synagogue in which some Jews were persuaded as well as *"a great many of devout Greeks, and not a few of the leading women"* (Acts 17:4). The phrase, *leading women*, referred no doubt to the wives of the leaders of the city, three of whom may have seen their husbands come to Christ and later become Paul's traveling companions on his missionary journey.

Very quickly the unbelieving Jews stirred up the mobsters in the market, attacking the house of Jason where the mission team had been staying. Not finding the team, they dragged Jason and some of the believers before the rulers or politarchs of the city, accusing them of harboring *"these men who have turned the world upside down . . . acting against the decrees of Caesar, saying that there is 'another king, Jesus.'"* The rulers only required a promise from Jason and his friends and let them go, whereupon the believers hustle away Paul and Silas by night to Berea, the closest town not on the Egnatian Road (Acts 17:5-10).

This political response in Thessalonica is unusually mild, considering the intense opposition by the Jews, and particularly the severity of the accusation. Such could have been the case because three of the "politarchs" may have become believers. In 1876, the city officials of Thessalonica, (the modern "Salonica"), decided to tear down an ancient arch called the "Vardar Gate" that spanned the Egnatian Road. Upon doing so, they discovered inscriptions of the names of the ancient city's politarchs dating to the period

Paul entered the city.[56] Among the names were **Sopater**, **Secundus** and **Gaius**,[57] the same names included later in Acts as traveling companions of Paul from that area (Acts 19:29, 20:4).

§ **Berea, not a capital but a large Macedonian city.** Paul again deviates from his Kingdom Commission, fleeing persecution and finding refuge in Berea (Acts 17:10). According to Cicero it was an "out of the way city."[58] Here Paul enters the synagogue and finds the Jews more willing to search the Scriptures for themselves than those in Thessalonica. *"Many of them therefore believed, with not a few Greek **women of high standing as well as men**"*(Acts 17: 12). When the antagonistic Jews from Thessalonica found Paul in Berea and stirred up the crowds there, the brethren quickly sent him away to the sea, and then accompanied him to Athens.

🏛 **Athens. The Capital of Greece**[59] Athens was "the intellectual metropolis of the ancient world – the mother of arts and eloquence."[60] Though Paul is alone here, he still continued his usual proclamation of the gospel. He first went to the synagogue, seemingly with no success, then to the market where certain Epicurean and Stoic philosophers met him and invited him to speak at the Areopagus. There he gave his great message beginning with the inscription on the altar *"TO THE UNKNOWN GOD."* He boldly proclaimed the gospel truths about the Almighty God, the Creator and Savior of our souls to those with no Scriptural background (Acts 17:16-31).

Acts records some who believed and one in particular with the title of a leader, **Dionysius the Areopagite,** a member of the Areopagus Court (Acts 17:34).

🏛 **Corinth. The Capital of Achaia.**[61] The strategy of Paul's Kingdom Commission impacting an entire city seems to be very effective in Corinth. Acts 18:8 states, *"Then **Crispus the ruler of the synagogue,** believed on the Lord with ull his household. And **many of the Corinthians, hearing, believed** and were baptized."* (NKJV) The influence of the believing ruler of the synagogue was instrumental in the conversion of many in Corinth.

🏛 **Ephesus. The Capital of Asia Minor.**[62] Paul spends more time here than any other city, establishing his flagship church and teaching in the school of Tyrannus. At this significant capital city, Luke records Paul's continuing commitment to fulfill his Kingdom Commission and his resolution to go to the Imperial Capital of the world. *"Paul resolved in the Spirit to pass through Macedonia and Achaia and go to Jerusalem, saying, 'After I have been there, I must also see Rome'"* (Acts 19:21). Christ confirmed His strategy as we see next.

🏛 **Jerusalem. The Initial Capital.** And the night following, the Lord stood by him and said, *"Be of good courage, Paul; for as you have testified of Me in Jerusalem, so must you bear witness also in Rome"* (Acts 23:11). We must not miss the Kingdom Commission here. Both the religious capital of the world and the imperial capital of the world are specifically and strategically targeted by God Himself.

▥ **Caesarea. The Roman Capital of Judea.**[63]   On his way to Rome, Paul spent two years in Caesarea, some twenty years after the centurion had been won to Christ by Peter. **In fact, this capital city and Jerusalem are the only two cities to be evangelized by all three of the evangelists.** Paul again fulfilled his commission to witness to "*kings*" as he declared the truth to **Governors Felix,** (Acts 23:24-25:14) **Festus** and **King Agrippa** as well as all the commanders and prominent men of that strategic capital (Acts 25:23-26:32). And it is here that he appeals to **Caesar** (Acts 25:10-12, 2 Timothy 4:16, 17). On his journey to Rome when shipwrecked on Malta, Paul witnesses to the leader, Publius, and heals his father (Acts 28:7-9).

▥ **Rome. The Imperial Capital.**   During the fearful storm at sea en route to Rome, Paul encouraged his shipmates, "*For there stood by me this night an angel of the God to whom I belong and whom I serve, saying, 'Do not be afraid, Paul; you must be brought before Caesar; and indeed God has granted you all those who sail with you'*" (Acts 27:23-24). Paul is promised the lives of all his shipmates as well as the divine confirmation to witness to the emperor. Later from Rome, Paul includes greetings from believers among Caesar's household (Philippians 4:22).

There are ten times throughout the book of Acts when Christ supernaturally intervenes:

1) Stephen is given a supernatural vision as he proclaims the truth to the Sanhedrin, the ruling body of Israel: *"Behold, I see the heavens opened and the Son of Man standing at the right hand of God"* (Acts 7:56).

2) Phillip is supernaturally directed to go in the desert to witness to *"an Ethiopian a eunuch, a court official of Candice, queen of the Ethiopians, who was in charge of all her treasure"* (8:26-27).

3) The prominent Jewish leader and member of the Sanhedrin, Saul, the arrestor of Christians, is supernaturally arrested and blinded by the Risen Lord on the road to Damascus (9:3-8).

4) Later Saul is personally commissioned by Christ through Ananias to *"bear my name before the Gentiles and kings and the children of Israel"* (9:15).

5) Peter is supernaturally directed to witness to *"Cornelius, a centurion, an upright and God-fearing man, who is well spoken of by the whole Jewish nation"* in the Roman Capital of Caesarea (10:10-22).

6) The first mission team is supernaturally sent out of a capital city, and they go first to the Island of Cyprus where they win their first king, Sergius Paulos, and then continue to evangelize capitals (13:2).

7) Paul is supernaturally directed away from Asia and Bithynia but toward Macedonia, leading him along the Apian Way, through the capital of Macedonia and eventually to the imperial capital of Rome (16:6-10).

8) The Lord personally encourages Paul to stay in the capital city of Corinth, "*for I have many in this city who are My people*" (18:9-10).

9) The night following the conflict with the Sanhedrin, the Lord stood by Paul's side saying, "*Take courage, for as you have testified to the facts about Me in Jerusalem, so you must testify also in Rome*" (23:11).

10) Again Paul is supernaturally encouraged amidst a life-threatening storm, "*Do not be afraid, Paul; you must stand before Caesar. And behold, God has granted you all those who sail with you*" (27:24).

Every case of supernatural intervention in Acts points to winning leaders!

Furthermore, Luke bookends both of his books, Luke and Acts, emphasizing capitals and leaders, beginning each book by writing to Theophilus, the governor, and ending with the Kingdom Commission in Luke, and its fulfillment in the end of Acts. F.F. Bruce says of Luke,

"His first volume is in essence a record of the apostolic witness to Jesus' ministry of word, deed, suffering and triumph. His second volume takes up… after the resurrection of Jesus and carries it on for some thirty years; he traces the progress of Christianity from Judea to Rome, and ends with the chief herald of the gospel proclaiming it at the heart of the empire with the full acquiescence of the imperial authorities."[64]

⌂ Spain. Paul's strategic destination

In what way would Paul's Kingdom Commission include Spain (Romans 15:28)? John MacArthur says, "Spain was on the far western side of the continent and had become a major center of commerce and culture, made accessible by way of the renowned Roman roads. Ruins of impressive Roman architecture still exist there today. That province had produced such outstanding men as Martial, famous for his epigrams; the poet Lucan; the notable orator Quintilian; and the greatest Spaniard in the Roman Empire, Seneca, the notable statesman and Stoic philosopher who tutored Nero and was prime minister of the Empire."[65] It seems Paul wanted to win the man who trained the Emperors.

The most renowned scholar and archaeologist of the travels of Paul, William Ramsey, said of him,

"Of all the men of the first century, incomparably the most influential was the Apostle Paul. No other man exercised anything like so much power as he did in molding the future of the Empire. Among the Imperial ministers of the period, there appeared none that had any claim to the name of statesman except Seneca; and

Seneca fell as far short of Paul in practical influence and intellectual insight as he did in moral character."[66]

To summarize: Fifteen of the nineteen cities evangelized by Paul were capitals (or the equivalent of a capital in the case of Philippi). What about the other four? The exceptions prove the rule. Barnabas was the leader of the mission team when they went to his home city, Salamis, and the three others were cities to which they *"fled"* due to intense persecution – Lystra, Derbe and Berea.

Conclusively Paul chose to evangelize capitals, being commissioned specifically by the Lord to win *kings*, which he would only find in capital cities. In fact, he was so successful in fulfilling his Kingdom Commission, that after evangelizing about half of the capital cities of his missionary journeys, the opposition complained, *"These men who have turned the world upside down have come here also"* (Acts 17:6).

McKee Adams in his excellent work *Biblical Backgrounds*, concludes that the primary relationship between the cities Paul evangelized was their political importance:

> "The importance of these cities related, in the first instance, to their political status. Without exception every city named here occupied the position of an administrative center for the surrounding territory. In the cases of Antioch in Syria, Tarsus, Ephesus, and Corinth, we are actually dealing with provincial capitals. Rome, of course, stands out as the imperial center."[67]

Dr. James Kelso discovers the same strategy and relates it even more clearly in his book, *An Archaeologist follows the Apostle Paul*, in the chapter titled, *Paul's Strategy of World Evangelism*, he says,

> "Provincial capitals such as Antioch gave Paul his strategy for world evangelism. Into these cities in the course of the year came all the imperial, provincial, and local politicians. Here was the highest central law court for the province; only a few matters could be appealed from this court to the emperor. As the business center of the province, the capital would be frequently visited by all the important businessmen, if it were not their permanent headquarters. The central tax office for the whole province was located in the capital. Furthermore numerous religious shrines were centered in these capitals and religious holidays called in their devout followers from the whole province several times each year. Thus all the most influential people of every phase of life would be in the provincial capital at least several times a year. Paul's missionary program was to evangelize these provincial capitals of the empire and sooner or later get to Rome itself."[68]

William Taylor, the pastor who first opened my eyes to Paul's strategy, may have best emphasized this Kingdom Commission in his summary of the life of Paul, "We see in the book of the Acts of the Apostles, how, from one center of influence to another, Paul went on and up, until at length he made his way to Rome, and had his converts both in the 'palace of the Caesars' and in the legions of the empire."[69]   Thus, Paul, writing from Rome could say, *"all the saints greet you, especially those of Caesar's household"* (Philippians 4:22).

Taylor continues:

> "[Paul] recognized in Rome the great heart of the world, and he was eager to take that for Christ. ...At Rome, therefore, he would be in direct communication with those who molded the destinies of the world.
>
> ...He had but one life to spend for his Master, and he sought to make the most of that by placing himself in those localities in which he could meet men from the remotest points, and from which the currents of travel would carry his doctrines to the limits of imperial civilization. Therefore we find him at Antioch, at Ephesus, at Thessalonica, at Corinth; and therefore also he desired to preach the gospel to them who were in Rome.
>
> ...What Jerusalem was to Palestine, during the Passover week, that Rome was to all the world throughout the year; and just as to-day, standing in the office of the Western Union, one may send telegraphic messages east and west and north and south, girdling the globe within a few hours, so in the imperial city, one might send his influence, not so rapidly, but just as really, throughout the entire domain over which the Roman standards waved."[70]

Thus, these commenters all recognize not only the strategic importance of Rome as an imperial city, but in fulfillment of Christ's Kingdom Commission, Rome was simply the final destination in Paul's missionary strategy to disciple the nations through the evangelization of capital cities.

Paul's every action and expression reflect this passion and sacrificial commitment: *"Now I want you to know, brethren, that my circumstances have turned out for the greater progress of the gospel, so that my imprisonment in the cause of Christ has become well known throughout the whole praetorian guard and to everyone else"* (Philippians 1:12-13, NASB). Taylor again comments: "These soldiers were always in communication with distant places; they were liable to be sent on important missions to far away provinces, and, converted themselves, they would become in the most natural way missionaries of the gospel of Christ wherever they went."[71]

Taylor finally directs himself to every disciple of Christ with a concluding application from 1 Corinthians 1:27-29:

"Now, leaving out of view the lesson which Paul's plan of labor furnishes to missionaries and evangelists, bidding them as it does to devote themselves to the great cities, and leave the converts in them to attend to the wants of the surrounding districts, what a comfort is there in all this to those among us who are eagerly yearning to reach some place of pre-eminent usefulness in the world!"

"God chose what is foolish in the world to shame the wise; God chose what is weak in the world to shame the strong; God chose what is low and despised in the world, even things that are not, to bring to nothing things that are, so that no human being might boast in the presence of God"

"The Apostle had proved the power of the gospel in other places, and it was not because he trusted in himself, but because he had confidence in the truth about Christ, and in the God who had commissioned him to preach it, that he desired to bring it face to face with the most potent forces which the world had ever seen."[72]

May this passion and sacrificial commitment continue in our churches today, as we, the *"foolish,"* *"weak"*, and *"despised"* seek to win the *"wise"* and *"strong"* for Christ.

IV. The Kingdom Commission and the Church Today

The practical question then arises: Did Paul's Kingdom Commission of strategic ministry to leaders die with him, or does Christ command the Church of today with the same commission? Or to put it another way, Does the exhortation of Paul to the church found in our text, I Timothy 2:1-4, represent the same commission of Christ to His church found in Matthew 28:19-20 and Acts 1:8, the same kingdom commission that Christ gave to Paul in Act 9:15? **This question is vitally important.** If all the commissions of Christ express the same directive to disciple the nations by reaching leaders, and Paul in this final New

Testament commission to Timothy passes on his Kingdom Commission to the Church, then we are still responsible for this strategic emphasis on evangelism and missions in our churches today.

God's plan in the Old Testament for the glory of His name among the Gentiles involved the direct proclamation of His truth by the prophets to kings and leaders of Israel and the Gentile nations. With the advent of the New Covenant and its emphasis on Christ as the Savior of the World, His commission found in Matthew 28:19-20 requires a strategy that has to include leaders when He commands His Church to *"disciple all the nations."* The Great Commission found in Acts 1:8 centers on capital cities: *Jerusalem, Samaria, and the end of the earth,* (which would be interpreted as Rome). This Kingdom Commission is reinforced by Christ when He personally commissions Paul as the Apostle to the Gentiles in Acts 9:15, *"He is a chosen instrument of Mine, to bear My name before the Gentiles and kings and the children of Israel."* The final commission in 1 Timothy 2:1-4 repeats the command to evangelize *"all men, of kings and all who are in authority"* through prayer and knowledge of the truth.

Now carefully compare these commissions. The two final commissions are tied together with a three-fold cord, completely omitting any geographical emphasis. The three people groups of Paul's original commission, *"Gentiles and kings and the children of Israel",* are simply restated as *"all men, kings and all who are in authority."* Thus, clearly providing the universal emphasis (*"all men"*) found in

Paul's original commission ("*Gentiles and the children of Israel*") and the Great Commission ("*all the nations*"), but especially emphasizing the importance of ministering to leaders ("*all who are in authority*"). The "*kings*" of Paul's original commission crescendo with a double emphasis on "*kings and all who are in authority*" when he passes his Kingdom Commission on to the Church. Paul clearly entrusts the Church with precisely the same people groups, but with a greater strategic emphasis on leaders, helping the church understand that the "*all men*" must never be construed to neglect "*all who are in authority*", but instead they are to be a strategic priority which the Church of that day as well as today is prone to overlook. **Though "*all who are in authority*" indicates that none are to be left out or excluded, it seems leaders are often the most unreached people group.**

In context, notice that Paul states that this Kingdom Commission entrusted to the Church is the strategic summary of his ministry, "*For this I was appointed a preacher and an apostle (I am telling the truth, I am not lying) as a teacher of the Gentiles [Nations] in faith and truth.*" (1 Timothy 2:7) As a final capstone to this Old and New Testament emphasis, it is also worth noting that four of the seven churches addressed in Revelation 1-3 were also located in capital cities.[73] And regarding God's glorious eternal capital, Jerusalem, "*The nations will walk by it's light, and the kings of the earth will bring their glory into it. In the daytime (for there will be no night there) its gates will never be closed; and they will bring the glory and honor of the nations into it*" (Revelation 21:24-26).

The biblical evidence regarding the responsibility of the Church to her governmental leaders has grown into a virtual Mount Everest as we have gleaned passages from Genesis to Revelation. It is demonstrated in the Preaching of the Prophets, the Ministry of the Messiah and the Clarity of the Commissions, with each one building on the other through the progressive revelation of God's truth.

Practical Applications

This leadership emphasis should influence the way we approach every part of the ministry in the Church: our priorities, our prayer, our responsibility to our government, our pursuit of peace and religious freedom, our methods in missions, our modes of evangelism, our passion for the lost, and our presentation of the gospel, to name just a few. No doubt this strategy can be applied, as Paul did, to many other areas in ministry. Can you think of anything more spiritually strategic for the kingdom than winning and discipling our leaders? **Have you sought to develop a strategy from Scripture to win your community, your city, your state, your nation and especially Christ's command to "*disciple all the nations*"?** What might happen in our nation if those in every Bible-believing church utilized these powerful means of grace: prayer and ministry of the Word, both publicly in their services and privately in their homes, praying for our leaders and seeking to minister the Word to them personally.

Our Scriptural responsibility to our government, in sum, is to pray for our government leaders and seek to win and disciple them for Christ. Historically from the time of the early church up through and following the Reformation, prayer for governmental leaders was practiced in the common worship of the church: "The practice of praying for our rulers and officials is mandated in the Episcopal prayer books, but often forgotten in fundamentalist churches."[74]

As we will see especially in chapter three, the church fathers were committed to pray for their political leaders even in the context of persecution. Their witness and ministry of the Word is documented by Phillip Schaff in his *History of the Christian Church*, who states: "The oldest post-Apostolic witness is Clement of Rome who wrote about AD 95: 'Paul... having come to the limit of the West and borne witness before the magistrates departed from the world and went to the holy place, having furnished the sublimest model of endurance.'"[75] Schaff observes the same pattern in later church history:

"The missionaries aimed first at the conversion of the rulers of the barbarian races of Western and Northern Europe. Augustine, with his thirty monks, was provided by Pope Gregory with letters to princes, and approached first King Ethelbert and Queen Bertha in Kent. Boniface leaned on the pope and Charles Martel. The conversion of Clovis decided the religion of the Franks. The Christian rulers became at once the patrons of the church planted among their subjects, and took Constantine and Theodosius for their models." [76]

In the same vein, John Calvin dedicated most of his works on the Old and New Testaments to European Kings and Dukes and political leaders, and even the early translators of his works into English did the same.[77] In his *Institutes of the Christian Religion*, which he dedicates in exile to Francis, King of France, he says to his king: "Even now, when exiled from our home, we nevertheless cease not to pray for all prosperity to your person and your kingdom."[78]

These godly men of Church history were simply following the example of Christ who not only emphasized the need to pray for government leaders, but also personally exemplified great boldness in witnessing to them as well. R.F. Horton says of Christ, "His confession before Pilate became the model, the motive, and the power of all the confessions which His followers make for him." [79]

In 1 Timothy 6:12-13, Paul ends this epistle exalting Christ as the ultimate example of witnessing to His human king: *"Christ Jesus who witnessed the good confession before Pontius Pilate."* (NKJV) **The last person to whom Jesus Christ witnessed before His death was the king who ordered His execution.** Considering the reference in 2:1-4 to prayer for their salvation, Paul bookends this epistle with an emphasis on leaders with Christ as the greatest example of boldness in discipling political leaders.

The kind of boldness demonstrated by Jesus Christ in His witness to Pilate, is the example to which Paul directs the church's attention, using His full title: "*King of kings and Lord of lords*" (1 Tim. 6:15). He is all the more honored as "*King of kings and Lord of lords*" as our leaders (kings) bow their knee before Him and receive Him as Lord of their lives.

Maybe you are asking in your heart, "Will my prayers really make a difference **today** regarding our nation?" God certainly used prayer to make a difference in East Germany in our time – only a little over 20 years ago. In May of 1989 at Leipzig, East Germany in the historic Nicolai Kirche (St. Nicholas Church) in the country where the reformation had been introduced exactly 450 years earlier, a small group began to meet in one of the church's rooms to read the Sermon on the Mount and pray for peace. The group expanded and moved to a larger room and finally met in the church's nave, which began to fill up. Alarmed, the communist authorities sent officials to attend. They threatened the gatherers and temporarily jailed some. On prayer nights they blocked the city's nearest autobahn off-ramp. But the group continued to grow.

Then on October 9, 1989 some 2000 individuals crowded in to pray for peace, and another 10,000 gathered outside with candles in their hands, demonstrating their peaceful intent since the use of both hands to hold the candle and shield it from the wind, proved they could not hold rocks or weapons. Before his death, a member of the Communist government, Sindermann, said of that night: "We had planned everything. We were prepared for everything. But not for candles and prayers."

On November 9, precisely a month later, the Berlin Wall came down. Coincidence? I think not! This was the kind response of a caring, all-powerful God in answer to prayer.[80]

Reporters said that the wall came down that evening because a German TV reporter accidentally said that the wall had opened, when it was never on his script. The anticipation of the people was evidently so strong that everyone accepted his accidental report as factual. The guards believed the newsman and chose to leave and go home for the evening since the wall was supposed to be open. And the people so anticipated this answer to prayer that they suddenly flooded outside the wall and began to celebrate. That night they were granted their peace!

Endnotes

12 Email from a Virginia Delegate dated February 20, 2009, who will remain anonymous.

13 Genesis 14:22-23.

14 Genesis 18:22-33. (The homosexual lust in Sodom was so severe that the men, after trying to rape the angels sent to rescue Lot and his family, "*wore themselves out groping for the door*" after being struck with blindness, Genesis 19:11).

15 Daniel 5:18-21.

16 Hugh Martin, The Prophet Jonah, (Grand Rapids, Michigan: Baker Book House, 1979), 333.

17 The first phrase follows the Hebrew norm in writing. A summary statement is made first, involving the whole, then the details are explained. Thus, the passage should not be construed to imply that the people repented first and then the leaders because it strategically states how the people repented: "*from the greatest to the least of them*" (Jonah 3:5). Then specifically what is meant by "*from the greatest to the least of them*" in providing the repentance of the king and the decree from the king and his nobles (3:6-9).

18 E.P. Alldredge, *Forty Sermon Studies from the Book of Jonah* (Nashville, Tennessee: Broadman Press, 1942), 49.

19 Daniel 4:1-4.

20 Ezra 7:12, Ezekiel 26:7, Daniel 2:37.

21 Ezra 6:10.

22 Robert L. Thomas and F. David Farnell, *The Jesus Crisis* (Grand Rapids: Kregel Publications, 1998), 38-57.

23 Piper, 204.

24 The word "*end*" is the word from which we get our word "escatology," pointing to the climactic end in which God will reign. "The Greek language uses the term *eschatos* to designate the end-point of a continuously conceived succession of circumstances. ...In qualitative respects *eschatos* designates an extreme positive or negative intensification... the highest reaches its peak with kings ...In Aristotle the term denotes the conclusion of a logical path of thought and thus contributes to the systematization of the thought-process." Colin Brown, ed., *The New International Dictionary of New*

Testament Theology, Vol. 2, (Grand Rapids: Zondervan Publishing House, 1986), 55.

25 David S. Dockery, ed., *The New American Commentary,* vol. 26, *Acts* by John B Polhill (Nashville, Tennessee: B&H Publishing Group, 1992), 86.

26 A. T. Robertson, *Word Pictures in the New Testament,* vol. 3, *Acts of the Apostles* (Grand Rapids: Baker Book House, 1930), 11.

27 "The bounds of Jewish narrowness are to be burst one after another until the church is planted at Rome, and the capital of the empire where (to quote Irenaeus' words) 'all meet from every quarter' will represent *the uttermost part of the earth.*" Richard Belward Rackham, *The Acts of the Apostles* (Grand Rapids: Baker Book House, 1964), 8.

28 "Probably 'the ends (sing., "end" in the Gr. Text) of the earth' looks to Rome, the proud center of world civilization in the Apostolic Age, a significant distance from Jerusalem (more than 1,400 miles, as the crow flies)." John F. Walvoord and Roy B. Zuck, eds., *The Bible Knowledge Commentary,* New Testament volume, *Acts* by Stanley D. Toussaint (Colorado Springs: Victor Books, 1987), 354.

29 William Barclay, *The Acts of the Apostles* (Philadelphia, Pennsylvania: The Westminster Press, 1955), xviii.

30 William Taylor, *Paul the Missionary* (Grand Rapids: Baker Book House, 1909 reprint 1962), 489.

31 Leon Morris, ed., *Tyndale New Testament Commentaries,* vol. 5, *Acts, An Introduction and Commentary,* by I. Howard Marshall (Downers Grove, Il: InterVarsity Press, 1980, Reprint 2008), 27.

32 Walter A. Elwell, ed., *Baker Enclycopedia of the Bible,* vol. 2 (Grand Rapids, Baker Book House, 1988), 1345.

33 Henry H. Halley, *Halley's Bible Handbook,* 24th edition (Grand Rapids: Zondervan Publishing House, 1965), 579.

34 William Steuart McBernie, *The Search for the Twelve Apostles* (Wheaton, Illinois: Pyramid Publications for Tyndale House Publishers, 1973), 243.

35 Robert Young, *Young's Analytical Concordance to the Bible* (Grand Rapids: Wm. B. Eerdmans Publishing Company), 735.

36 J. McKee Adams, *Biblical Backgrounds* (Nashville, Tennessee: Broadman Press, 1965), 198-99.

37   Merrill F. Unger, *Unger's Bible Handbook* (Chicago: Moody Press, 1967), 578.

38   Unger, 578.

39   Ibid.

40   A. T. Robertson, *Word Pictures in the New Testament*, vol. 3, *Acts of the Apostles* (Grand Rapids: Baker Book House, 1930), 180.

41   A. Roberts, *The Ante-Nicene Fathers: Translations of the writings of the fathers down to A.D. 325*, vol. 5, *Fathers of the Third Century: Hippolytus, Cyprian, Novation*, Appendix (electronic edition of the Edinburgh edition, Oak Harbor: Logos Research Systems).

42   Robertson, 181.

43   William Taylor, *Paul the Missionary* (Grand Rapids: Baker Book House, 1962), 104.

44   Walter A. Elwell, ed., *Baker Encyclopedia of the Bible*, vol. 1 (Grand Rapids: Baker Book House, 1988), 120.

45   Taylor, 128.

46   Ibid, 134.

47   Ibid.

48   Elwell, Vol. 2, 1676.

49   G. Campbell Morgan, *Acts of the Apostles* (Westwood: Fleming H. Revell Company, n.d.), 378.

50   Taylor, 224-5.

51   In context, 1 Cor.9:19-23 is Paul's ministry statement regarding his willingness to relinquish all rights as a Jew, a Roman citizen, or even as an Apostle for the sake of the gospel: *19 For though I am free from all, I have made myself a servant to all, that I might win more of them. 20 To the Jews I became as a Jew, in order to win Jews. To those under the law I became as one under the law (though not being myself under the law) that I might win those under the law. 21 To those outside the law I became as one outside the law (not being outside the law of God but under the law of Christ) that I might win those outside the law. 22 To the weak I became weak, that I might win the weak. I have become all things to all people, that by all means I might save some. 23 I do it all for the sake of the gospel, that I may share with them in its blessings.* For further study on the topic of political involvement, see *"Christians and Politics,"* by MacArthur: http://www.gty.org/resources/articles/a124/

52 Robertson, 250.

53 Taylor, 243

54 Ibid.

55 Halley, 574.

56 Simon J. Kistamaker, *Exposition of the Acts of the Apostles*, New Testament Commentary (Grand Rapids: Baker Book House, 1990), 617.

57 Everett F. Harrison, ed., *The Greek New Testament*, vol. 2, *Acts, Romans, Corinthians* by Henry Alford (Chicago: Moody Press, 1958), 188.

58 Unger, 588.

59 Adams, 204.

60 Taylor, 259.

61 Adams, 211.

62 Charles F. Pfeiffer, *Baker's Bible Atlas* (Grand Rapids: Baker Book House, 1961), 297.

63 Halley, 579.

64 F.F. Bruce, *Commentary on the Book of Acts* (Grand Rapids, Michigan: Wm. B. Eerdmans Publishing Co., 1979), 20.

65 John MacArthur, *The MacArthur NT Commentary: Romans 9-16* (Chicago: Moody Press, 1994), 344.

66 William M. Ramsay, *Pauline and Other Studies in Early Christian History* (Grand Rapids, Michigan: Baker Book House, 1970), 53.

67 Adams, 196.

68 James L. Kelso, *An Archaeologist follows the Apostle Paul* (Waco, Texas: Word Books Publishers, 1970), 38.

69 William M. Taylor, *Daniel the Beloved* (1878 reprint; Greenville, South Carolina: Ambassador Productions, Ltd., 1997), 52.

70 William M. Taylor, *The Limitations of Life and Other Sermons* (New York: Eaton and Mains, 1879), 265-267.

71 Taylor, *Paul the Missionary*, 490.

72 Taylor, *The Limitations of Life and Other Sermons,* 268.

73 *Rose Book of Bible Charts, Maps and Time Lines* (Torrance, California: Rose Publishing, 2005), 107.

74 Gordon H. Clark, *The Pastoral Epistle,* (Jefferson, Maryland: The Trinity Foundation, 1983), 30.

75   Phillip Schaff, *History of the Christian Church,* vol. 1, *Apostolic Christianity* (Grand Rapids, Michigan: Wm B. Eerdmans Publishing Company, 1910), 332.

76   Ibid., vol. IV, *Mediaeval Christianity,* 386.

77   The **Genesis** Commentary introducing the series on the Old Testament is dedicated by John Calvin to "The Most Illustrious Prince, **Henry,** Duke of Vendome, Heir to the Kingdom of Navarre" at "Geneva, July 31, 1563." To which is footnoted "Afterwards the celebrated **Henry IV of France**, a brave and noble-spirited Prince, addicted, however to the frivolities, and enslaved by the licentiousness of the age. He was induced to renounce his Protestant principles for the Crown of France; and at length fell by the hand of an assassin, on account of his tolerance towards the Huguenots." The second footnote about Henry adds: "He was born in 1553, and therefore in 1563, the date of this dedication, he was ten years old." John Calvin, *Commentaries on the First Book of Moses called Genesis,* Vol. 1, Trans. John King, 1st translator, Thomas Tymme (Grand Rapids, Michigan: Baker Books, Reprint 1999), Calvin: xlv, Tymme: xli. 1578. Translation dedicated by Thomas Tymme to "The Right Honorable, my Verie Good Lorde Ambrose, Earle of Warwicke, Baron Lisle, Maister of Her Maiestie's Ordinance, Knight of the Most Noble Order of the Garter, and one of Her Highnesse Priuie Counsell, and to the Right Honorable Ladie His Wife, Encrease of Honor, and True Knowledge in Christ Iesvs."

The **Isaiah** Commentary is dedicated by Calvin to "His Serene Highness, **Edward Sixth, King of England**, &c. **A Truly Christian Prince.**" At "Geneva, 25th December, 1550." John Calvin, *Commentary on the Prophet Isaiah,,* Vol. 1, Trans. Rev. William Pringle, 1st translator, Clement Cotton, (Grand Rapids, Michigan: Baker Books, Reprint 1999), Calvin: xix, Cotton: x. Translation, January 15 of the year of Queen Elizabeth's Corronation by Clement Cotton to "The High and Mightie Prince, **Henrie, Prince of Great Brittaine**, Sonne and Heire Apparent to our Soueraigne Lord, James King of Great Brittaine, &c. **and** to the Most Noble and Vertvovs **Princessse, the Lady Elizabeths** Grace, His Hignesse Most Dear Sister; all Honor and Happinesse with eternall glorie through Christ Iesvs."

The **Jeremiah** Commentary is dedicated by Calvin to "The Most Illustrious Prince, **D. Frederick, Lord Palatine of the Rhine, and Elector of the Roman Empire**, etc," at "Geneva, July 23, 1563." John Calvin, *Commentary on the Prophet Jeremiah and the*

*Lamentations,,*Vol. 1, Trans. Rev. John Owen, 1st translator, Clement Cotton, (Grand Rapids, Michigan: Baker Books, Reprint 1999), Calvin: xvi, Cotton: xiv. Translation dedicated by Clement Cotton to "The Noble and Vertvovs Lady, The Lady Lvcie, Countesse of Bedford: And to the Right Honorable and Highly Honoured Lady, The Lady Ann Harrington, Barrones: mercy and peace be multiplied."

The **Daniel** Commentary is dedicated by Calvin to "All the pious worshippers of God who desire the Kingdom of Christ to be rightly constituted in France." At "Geneva, August 19, 1561." John Calvin, *Commentaries on the Book of Prophet Daniel,*Vol. 1, Trans. Thomas Myers, 1st translator, Bartholomew Vincent (Grand Rapids, Michigan: Baker Books, Reprint 1999), Calvin: lxiv.

The **Minor Prophets** Commentaries are dedicated by Calvin to "The Most Serene and Most Mighty **King Gustavus, the king of the Goths and Vandals**." At "Geneva, January 26, 1559." At "Geneva, January 26, 1559." To which is footnoted "**Gustavus was the King of Sweden,** the inhabitants of which were then called Goths and Vandals. He was the first king of that name in Sweden, and had the surname of Vasa. He was born in 1490, and was a descendant of the royal family of Sweden. He delivered the kingdom from the attempted usurpation of Christian II of Denmark, was made king in 1523, abolished Popery, and introduced Lutheranism in 1530, and died at the age of seventy, in 1560, the year following the date of this Epistle." John Calvin, *Commentaries on the Twelve Minor Prophets,* Vol. 1, Trans. Rev. John Owen, 1st translator, John Budaeus (Grand Rapids, Michigan: Baker Books, Reprint 1999), Calvin: xvii.

The **Matthew** Commentary included in his Harmony of the Gospels is dedicated by Calvin to "The Very Noble and Illustrious Lords, **The Burgomasters and Council of the Noble City of Frankfort**" at "Geneva, 1st of August, M.D.L.V." John Calvin, *Commentary on a Harmony of the Evangelists, Matthew, Mark, and Luke,*Vol. 1, Trans. Rev. William Pringle, 1st translator, Eusebius Paget (Grand Rapids, Michigan: Baker Books, Reprint 1999), Calvin: xxix, Paget: xxv. 1584 Translation dedicated by Eusebius Paget to "The Right Honorable Francis, Earl of Bedford, of the Noble Order of the Garter, Knight, one of the Lords of Her Majesty's Most Hon. Privy Council; grace and peace from God, with the increase of that true honor which is from God, and lasteth for ever."

The **John** Commentary is dedicated by Calvin to "The Truly Honorable and Illustrious Lords, the Syndics and **Council of Geneva, John Calvin supplicates from the Lord the spirit of wisdom and firmness, and a prosperous administration.**" At "Geneva, 1st of January, 1553." John Calvin, *Commentary on the Gospel according to John*, Vol. 1, Trans. Rev. William Pringle, 1st translator, Christopher Fetherstone (Grand Rapids, Michigan: Baker Books, Reprint 1999), Calvin: 15, Fetherstone: 13. Translation dedicated by Christopher Fethersone to "The Right Honorable The Lord Robt. Dvdley, Earle of Leycester, Baron of Denbigh, Maister of the Horse to the Queene's Maiestie, Knight of the Noble Order of the Garter, and one of the Queen Maistie's Most Honorable Priuie Counsel, Chancelour of the Most Famous Universitie of Oxford."

The **Acts** Commentary is dedicated by Calvin to "The Most Renowned Prince, The **Lord Nicolas Radziwill**, Duke in Olika, County Palatine of Vilna, Chief Marshal, and **Head Chancellor of the Great Dukedom of Lithuania**, etc.," "At Geneva, the 1st of August, 1560." John Calvin, *Commentary upon the Acts of the Apostles,*, Vol. 1, Trans. Henry Beveridge, Esq, 1st translator, Christopher Fetherstone (Grand Rapids, Michigan: Baker Books, Reprint 1999), Calvin: xv, Fetherstone: ix. 1585 Translation dedicated by Christopher Fetherstone to "The Right Honorable The Lord Henry, Earl of Huntington, Lord Hastings, etc., Knight of the Most Honorable Order of the Garter, and Lord President of the Queen's Majesty's Counsel established in the North Parts."

The **Romans** Commentary is dedicated by Calvin to "**Simon Grynaeus, A man worthy of all honor.**" At "Strasburgh, 18th October 1539." To which is footnoted "The account given of Grynaeus by Watkins in his Biographical Dictionary, taken from Moreri, is the following: 'A learned German, born at Verigen, in Hohenzolllern, in 1493. He studied at Vienna, after which he became Rector of the School at Baden, but **was thrown into prison for espousing the Lutheran doctrines**. However, he recovered his liberty, and went ot Heidelberg, afterwards to Basil, and in 1531, he visited England. In 1536 he returned to Basil and died there in 1540.'" John Calvin, *Commentary on the Epistle of Paul the Apostle to the Romans*, Trans. Rev. John Owen (Grand Rapids, Michigan: Baker Books, Reprint 1999), Calvin: xxiii.

The **I Corinthians** Commentary is dedicated by Calvin to "That Illustrious Man, **James of Burgundy, Master of Falais and Breda**." At "Geneva, 24ᵗʰ January 1546." The **2 Corinthians** Commentary is dedicated by Calvin to "**Lord Galliazus Caracciolus: A Nobleman,** distinguished still more by eminent virtues than by illustrious descent, only son and rightful heir of the Marquis of Vico." On "24ᵗʰ January 1556, ten years after this Commentary was first published." John Calvin, *Commentaries on the Epistles of Paul the Apostle to the Corinthians,* Trans. Rev. John Pringle, 1ˢᵗ translator, Thomas Tymme (Grand Rapids, Michigan: Baker Books, Reprint 1999), Calvin: 29, 33, Tymme: 26. Translation by Thomas Tymme to "The Most Reverend Father in God, and his singular good Lord, Edmond, by the grace of God, Archbishop of Canterburie, Primate and Metropolitane of all England."

The **Galatians** Commentary is dedicated by Calvin to "The Most Illustrious **Prince Christopher, Duke of Wirtemberg, Earl of Montbeliard.**" At "Geneva, 1ˢᵗ February 1548." John Calvin, *Commentaries on the Epistle of Paul to the Galatians,1 & 2 Thessalonians,* Trans. Rev. William Pringle, 1ˢᵗ translator, Auchtebarder (Grand Rapids, Michigan: Baker Books, Reprint 1999), Calvin: ix, 234, 308.

The **1 Thessalonians** Commentary is dedicated by Calvin to **one of his former teachers,** "**Maturinus Corderius,** a men ot eminent piety and learning, **principal of the College of Lausanne.**" At "Geneva, 17ᵗʰ February 1550." The **2 Thessalonians** Commentary is dedicated by Calvin to **his personal doctor** "That Distinguished Man, **Benedict Textor, Physician.**" At "Geneva, 1ˢᵗ July 1550."

The **1 Timothy** Commentary is dedicated by Calvin to "The Most Nobel and **Truly Christian Prince, Edward, Duke of Somerset,** Earl of Hertfore, &c., **Protector of England and Ireland,** and Royal Tutor." At "Geneva, 25ᵗʰ July 1556." John Calvin, *Commentaries on the Epistles to Timothy, Titus and Philemon,* Trans. Rev. William Pringle, 1ˢᵗ translator, Auchtebarder (Grand Rapids, Michigan: Baker Books, Reprint 1999), Calvin: ix, 275.   The **Titus** Commentary is dedicated by Calvin to **the two men who persuaded him to minister in Geneva,** "Two Eminent Servants of Christ, **William Farell and Peter Viret,** his dearly beloved brethren and colleagues." At "Geneva, 29ᵗʰ November 1549."

The **Hebrews** Commentary is dedicated by Calvin to "The Most Mighty and Most Serene Prince, **Sigismund Augustus**, by the grace of God, the **King of Poland, Great Duke of Lithuania, Russia, Prussia, and Lord and Heir of Moscovy**, etc." At "Geneva, May 23, 1549." John Calvin, *Commentaries on the Epistle of Paul the Apostle to the Hebrews*, Trans. Rev. John Owen, 1st translator, Clement Cotton (Grand Rapids, Michigan: Baker Books, Reprint 1999), Calvin: xix, Cotton: xvi. Translation by Clement Cotton to "The Right Honorable Robert Earle of Salisburie, Vicount Cranbourne, Baron of Essendon, Principall Secretarie to the Kingss most excellent Maiestie, Master of the Court of Wardes and Liueries, and one of His Highnesse most Honorable Privie Counsell."

The Epistles of **1 & 2 Peter, James, Jude** Commentaries are dedicated by Calvin to "His Most Serene Highness, **Edward the Sixth, the King of England, the Lord of Ireland**, and a most Christian Prince." At "Geneva, Jan. 24, 1551." John Calvin, *Commentaries on the Catholic Epistles*, Trans. Rev. John Owen (Grand Rapids, Michigan: Baker Books, Reprint 1999), Calvin: xi.

78 John Calvin, *Institutes of the Christian Religion*, Trans. Henry Beveridge (Grand Rapids, Michigan, 1998 reprint), 19.

79 Prof. W. F. Adney, General Editor, *The Century Bible, The Pastoral Epistles Timothy and Titus*, by R. F. Horton (Edinburgh: T. C. & E. C. Jack), 136.

80 Compiled from various online sources.

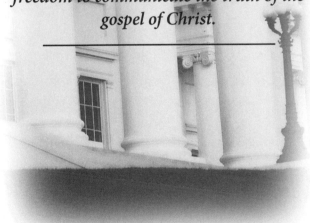

Paul provides a specific directive for external peace and religious freedom, at a time when the Church faced one of its worst periods of oppression and opposition. ...we must pray for our leaders, seeking their salvation.

We must not miss this link throughout Scripture between prayer and the ministry of the Word as God's means of salvation particularly for leaders, which provides for the peace of the Church resulting in greater freedom to communicate the truth of the gospel of Christ.

3

PEACE UNDER FIRE

*Prayer, the Peace of the Church
and Power of the Gospel*

The son of the royal family, his capital had been taken by a foreign invading army. Most likely at the tender age of 14, he was forced to become a slave. Not only did the invaders take the most valuable artifacts of the royal treasury, they took the children of the royal family in order to secure the loyalty of the country. Upon his arrival in the foreign capital, he was made a eunuch[81] robbing him of the hope of ever having a wife and family. To add insult to injury, he was deprived of his own name and given a name by his captors blasphemous to himself, to his God, and to his country.

Under this level of subjugation, he was expected to succeed, competing for three years in the emperor's college with the ablest youths and brightest minds of his day. One consolation was that most of his colleagues had suffered the same fate. Perhaps the highest pleasure anticipated was the meal time when they would be provided some of the best food in the land. Yet at the risk of his life and that of his friends, they requisitioned the president of the college for the opportunity to decline the delicious meat and wine. The college president, not willing to risk his life for these new students (since the emperor had personally determined the menu), set over them a man named Melzar, who would take personal responsibility for them while granting a vegetarian diet. Not only did they graduate at the top of their class, but they impressed the emperor, being ten times brighter than any of their classmates, and therefore were given the top leadership positions in the empire.

Soon however, not only were their excellent positions in jeopardy, but they were about to be executed. Arioch, the Captain of the King's Guard, was pounding on their door with a death sentence from the emperor. Such was the beginning of the tumultuous political lives of the great statesman, Daniel, and his three friends, Hananiah, Mishael, and Azaria. Clearly their need for peace and freedom to communicate the knowledge of God was paramount. Yet while facing certain death (humanly speaking) they overcame the impossible demands of the emperor, and found peace and opportunity to witness for God through prayer, which resulted in the salvation of their formerly evil emperor (Daniel 2:14-49).

Persecution of the church and prayer for peace

Most likely, at the time of Paul's writing of First Timothy, precisely the same danger threatened the Church through the irrational decree of execution by the command of their

Emperor. This threat began after Nero completed his master plan for the rebuilding of Rome, which he planned to rename "Neropolis." On July 18 of AD 64 (after which First Timothy was written according to many commentators[82]), to make way for his new city, Nero burned to the ground the imperial Capital of the Roman Empire.[83] However to his dismay, he found that the citizens of the city were furious at his rampant destruction. Nero had not only reduced to ashes the imperial museums, artifacts, and historical buildings, but members of many elite families and neighborhoods had perished, and their homes and possessions destroyed. Thus, the new class of homeless elite sought to have him deposed. Forced to find a scapegoat, Nero blamed the Christians, and suddenly the most horrendous worldwide persecution that the Church had ever known was upon them.

Immediately Christians in Rome were arrested by the hundreds and summarily crucified or tied up in the skins of wild beasts to be fed to ravenous dogs and other beasts in the amphitheater. Some were even nailed to poles, covered in pitch and burned alive to provide lighting for Nero's chariot races at night. Finding nowhere else to flee, the church went underground, and thus about 600 miles of catacombs began to be formed as the believers hid and buried their dead under the capital city of Rome.

Local persecution of the church and prayer for peace

The command to pray for governmental leaders and the resultant peace and freedom for the church was written to

Timothy pastoring in Ephesus[84]. To better understand the increasing danger facing the local church in Ephesus, we need to consider several other passages:

1) Paul had previously spoken regarding the region of Asia as more dangerous than any he had experienced:

    "For we do not want you to be ignorant, brothers, of the affliction we experienced in Asia. For we were so utterly burdened beyond our strength that we despaired of life itself. Indeed, we felt that we had received the sentence of death. But that was to make us rely not on ourselves but on God who raises the dead. He delivered us from such a deadly peril, and He will deliver us" (2 Corinthians 1:8-10).

2) In First Corinthians, he had shared with them his experiences in Ephesus, the capital:

    "Why am I in danger every hour? ...What do I gain if, humanly speaking, I fought with the beasts at Ephesus?" (1 Corinthians 15:30, 32).

    It is possible that Paul had been a gladiator in the arena and had won. Even if not, the text unquestionably relates intense persecution having taken place in Ephesus. As J.P. Lilley states, "There was no city in the world at this time in which greater hostility had been manifested towards Paul than in Ephesus."[85]

3) This may have been the reason why Paul later takes time to send messengers to have the elders of the Ephesian church meet him in Miletus, rather than going to meet them (Acts 20:17).

Additionally, there are at least four internal evidences within First Timothy pointing to intense persecution, likely following the burning of Rome:

1) Paul's purpose statement for writing the book of First Timothy. "*I am writing these things to you, hoping to come to you before long; but in case I am delayed, I write so that you will know how one ought to conduct himself in the household of God, which is the church of the living God, the pillar and support of the truth*" (1 Timothy 3:14-15 NASB). He plans to come soon, but specifically states that there may be an anticipated delay (due to a possible arrest or threat of persecution). If this is so, he wanted his flagship church to know what was essential for them in the life of the church. In this epistle, he covers the necessary instruction regarding the officers, members, and relationships within the church.

2) This is the only book where Paul names himself both as "*a persecutor, and injurious*" (1 Timothy 1:13). As a former persecutor, he would have experience dealing with persecution and persecutors. Ronald Cox says, "Added to this was the burning of Rome in 64 A.D. and the consequent persecution of Christians by Nero. Paul knew how to deal with the situation: the best way to combat persecution is to convert the persecutor (after all, he himself had been a persecutor and had been converted)."[86]

3) The mention of "*peaceable*" meaning "external peace", a word used only in 1 Timothy 2:2, would point to external

persecution motivating the prayers of the church to obtain that peace.

4) Here alone, Paul presents Jesus Christ before His persecutors as the ultimate example of boldness in witnessing to leaders, "*Who before Pontius Pilate witnessed a good confession*" (1 Timothy 6:13).

At this time, external peace for the free communication of the gospel would have been very precious to the church at Ephesus, and this recipe for peace was specifically provided in 1 Timothy 2:1-4 by Paul, the first persecutor of the Church. Meanwhile, Paul's flagship church in Ephesus had been led into trivialities by Hymenaeus and Alexander, mentioned in 1 Timothy 1, and was ill prepared for the persecution coming upon them.

Exposition of 1 Timothy 2:1-4 (author's translation)

"*I exhort therefore, first of all, to make supplications, prayers, intercessions and giving of thanks over all men, over kings and all those being in authority, in order that a **peaceable** and quiet life we may lead in all godliness and reverence. This is good and well pleasing before The Savior Our God, Whom all men He is willing to be saved and to come into the full knowledge of the truth.*"

Power packed in this short passage we find not only a fourfold emphasis on prayer as a first priority in evangelism emphasizing leaders, but prayer is also *the* primary means for that peace which provides the freedom and opportunity to communicate the saving gospel of Christ.

"In order that" introduces the result and purpose of this prayer. Peace to communicate the gospel, therefore, is the primary motivation and consequence of prayer, especially for leaders.

"Peaceable" (ηρεμον) – "Quiet, 'Tranquil", (tranquility arising from without)[87] This word is unique to the NT, used only here in the passage where prayer for leaders is most emphasized. We must understand this: Paul provides a specific directive for external peace and religious freedom, at a time when the Church faced one of its worst periods of oppression and opposition. The former leading persecutor is giving the Church the **only** clear and precise word for **external peace** in the entire New Testament, and at the time when the Church was vitally interested in external peace. If the Church today desires external peace and religious freedom, *we must pray* for our leaders, seeking their salvation.

The Development of Peace in Scripture

Peace is both commanded and promised to the upright in the Old Testament:

- Psalm 34:11-15 gives the imperative to *"seek peace and pursue it."*
- Psalm 37:11 *"The meek shall inherit the land and delight themselves in abundant peace"*
- Psalm 37:37 *"Mark the blameless man, and observe the upright; for the future of that man is peace."* (NKJV)

- Proverbs 16:7 *"When a man's ways please the Lord, He makes even his enemies to be at peace with him."*
- Isaiah 26:3 says it best, *"You keep him in perfect peace, whose mind is stayed on You, because he trusts in You."*

To drive us to greater prayer, we are admonished in the New Testament to pursue peace:

- Romans 12:18 *"If possible, so far as it depends on you, live peaceably with all."*
- Hebrews 12:14 *"Strive for peace with everyone, and for the holiness without which no one will see the Lord."*

The Example of Daniel

Without question, this pattern for peace was most clearly illustrated when God's people were deported to Babylon and were citizens of a foreign country. Jeremiah wrote a letter to the wicked world emperor, Nebuchadnezzar, to tell the people of God what would most please Him while they were in captivity in Babylon. Within that letter, Jeremiah sets the precedent for our passage, probably in the mind of Paul as he later writes of peace: *"And seek the peace of the city where I have caused you to be carried away captive, and pray to the Lord for it; for in its peace you will have peace."* (Jer. 29:7 NKJV)

It is possible that Daniel, the distinguished statesman in Babylon, may have even read this letter to Nebuchadnezzar. If true, we can better understand why he was so committed to prayer, facing lions in order to do so. Daniel committed himself to prayer three times each day, and acquired peace for his people throughout his lifetime, winning the hearts of the emperors of his day – Nebuchadnezzar, Cyrus, Darius and Artaxerxes (Daniel 4, 6:7, 25-28, Ezra 6:8-14).

Studying deeper into the practice of prayer three times a day, it is interesting that the only other place in the New Testament where we find this precise word, *"intercessions"* found in 1 Tim. 2:1 is later in 1 Timothy 4:3-5 in the context of *"foods which God created to be received with thanksgiving by those who believe and know the truth. For everything created by God is good, and nothing is to be rejected if it is received with thanksgiving; for it is made holy by the word of God and prayer* (intercession).*"* Intercession for the salvation of our leaders at the occasions of thanking God for our daily meals would be a wonderful way of fulfilling this directive from Christ for His church. Surely if Daniel could afford the time and suffer the political opposition to do so, it would not be too difficult for us. Since the busy statesman, Daniel, took the time to pray three times a day, shall we not at least attempt in a small way to be like Daniel and pray not only with thanksgiving, but also with grateful intercession for our leaders over our meals three times a day?

The Example of Esther

How did Esther obtain peace for God's people when they had been threatened so severely by wicked Haman? She and the Israelites acquired their peace and freedom through fasting and prayer (Esther 4:16), and God granted their request when she interceded for her people before the king. This deliverance is celebrated every year in March as Purim.

The Example of Stephen

More convincing examples of this pattern of peace and freedom through prayer are found in the New Testament. As stated earlier, Stephen prayed for his rulers as he died under the stones hurled from their hands, crying his last words, "*Lord, do not hold this sin against them.*" (Acts 7:60). **Jesus Christ personally answered his prayer from heaven and transformed Saul as the means by which the Church obtained peace and freedom for the advancement of the gospel.** "*So the church throughout all Judea, Galilee, and Samaria* **had peace** *and was being built up. And walking in the fear of the Lord and in the comfort of the Holy Spirit, it multiplied*" (Acts 9:31).

God used prayer to change the hearts of leaders, driving home the testimony of the gospel through Stephen's sermon and death. We must not miss this link throughout Scripture between prayer and the ministry of the Word as God's means of salvation particularly for leaders, which provides for the peace of the Church resulting in greater freedom to communicate the truth of the gospel of Christ. Thus the first link in this chain is prayer for leaders. The battle for Saul's heart was won and the peace for the Church was secured through prayer.

The Example of the Early Church Fathers

The early Church while under persecution understood the need to pray for their political leaders. In the late second or early third century, the theologian Tertullian wrote regarding 1 Timothy 2:1-3:

"Without ceasing, for all our emperors we offer prayer. We pray for life prolonged; for security to the empire; for protection to the imperial house; for brave armies, a faithful senate, a virtuous people, the world at rest, whatever, as man or Caesar, an emperor would wish. These things I cannot ask from any but God from whom I know I shall obtain them, both because He alone bestows them and because I have claims upon Him for their gift, as being a servant of His, rendering homage to Him alone.

Do you, then, who think that we care nothing for the welfare of Caesar, look into God's revelations, examine our sacred books, which we do not keep in hiding, and which many accidents put into the hands of those who are not of us. Learn from them that a large benevolence is enjoined upon us, even so far as to supplicate God for our enemies, and to beseech blessings on our persecutors. Who, then, are greater enemies and persecutors of Christians, than the very parties with treason against whom we are charged? Nay, even in terms, and most clearly, the Scripture says, 'Pray for kings, and rulers, and powers, that all peace may be with you.'"[88]

The second-century pastor and apologist, Theophilus of Antioch, summarizing 1 Peter 2:13-17 states:

"I will rather honor the king [than your gods], not, indeed, worshipping him, but praying for him. But God, the living and true God, I worship, knowing that the king is made by Him.

Honor the king, be subject to him, and pray for him with loyal mind; for if you do this, you do the will of God."[89]

Summarizing Romans 13:7-8 and 1 Timothy 2:3, Theophilus goes on to say:

"Moreover, concerning subjection to authorities and powers, and prayer for them, the divine Word gives us instructions, in order that *we may lead a quiet and peaceable life.* And it teaches us to render all things to all, *'honor to whom honor, fear to whom fear, tribute to whom tribute; to owe no man anything, but to love all.'*"[90]

Thus, the early Church Fathers also understood the importance of grateful intercessory prayer, especially for leaders, as the means given in Scripture for the external peace of the Church.

The Instruction of Calvin

Calvin, in his chapter on Civil Government in the *Institutes of the Christian Religion,* states in relation of the Church to the State: "The most celebrated passage of all is that in which Paul, admonishing Timothy, that prayers are to be offered up in the public assembly for kings, subjoins the reason, 'that we may live a quiet and peaceable life in all godliness and honesty' (1 Tim.ii:2). In these words, he recommends the condition of the church to their protection and guardianship."[91]

Internal Peace of the Church

Prayer also is the effectual means of tranquility *within* the Church. The next word, **quiet** (ησυξιον) means "quietness, stillness, silence (tranquility arising from within)."[92] It seems to picture a quiet and submissive respect and reverence for authority that honors that one in authority.

Uses of the word

The best picture from Scripture and the only other exact adjectival use of this word for internal peace in the New Testament is of the virtuous wife like Sarah in I Peter 3:4, describing "*a gentle and quiet spirit, which in God's sight is very precious.*"

Here are some noun uses of this same root word:

- Acts 22:2 "*And when they heard that he was addressing them in the Hebrew language, they became even more silent.*"
- 2 Thessalonians 3:11-12 "*For we hear that some among you walk in idleness, not busy at work, but busybodies. Now such persons we command and encourage in the Lord*

Jesus Christ to do their work **quietly** and to earn their own living."

- 1 Timothy 2:11-12 *"Let a woman learn **quietly** with all submissiveness. I do not permit a woman to teach or exercise authority over a man; rather, she is to remain **quiet**."*

Other verbal uses include:

- Luke 14:4 *"But they remained **silent**."*
- Luke 23:56 *"Then they returned and prepared spices and ointments. On the Sabbath they **rested** according to the commandment."*
- Acts 11:18 *"When they heard these things, they **fell silent**. And they glorified God, saying, 'Then to the Gentiles also God has granted repentance that leads to life.'"*
- Acts 21:14 *"Since he would not be persuaded, we **ceased** and said, 'Let the will of the Lord be done.'"*
- 1 Thessalonians 4:11-12 *"And aspire to live **quietly**, and to mind your own affairs, and to work with your own hands, as we instructed you, so that you may live properly before outsiders, and be dependent on no one."*

Importance of prayer and gratitude to maintain this peace in the Church

In the NT, this internal peace in the Church is tied to a loving and prayerful submission to pastoral care. Note the final words of Paul to the persecuted church in Thessalonica: *"We ask you, brothers, to respect those who labor among you and are over you in the Lord and admonish you, and to esteem them very highly in love because of their work. Be at peace among yourselves"* (1 Thessalonians 5:12-13).

The passage goes on to say, *"And we urge you, brothers, admonish the idle, encourage the fainthearted, help the weak, be patient with them all. See that no one repays anyone evil for evil, but always seek to do good to one another and to everyone. Rejoice always, pray without ceasing, give thanks in all circumstances; for this is the will of God in Christ Jesus for you."* (1 Thessalonians 5:14-18). Among the practical exhortations is continual, grateful prayer.

Paul, as a loving pastor, also requested such prayer:

- Romans 15:30 *"I appeal to you, brothers, by our Lord Jesus Christ and by the love of the Spirit, to strive together with me in your prayers to God on my behalf."*
- 2 Thessalonians 3:1 *"Finally, brothers, pray for us, that the Word of the Lord may speed ahead and be honored, as happened among you."*

Importance of our personal peace with God

Prayer also provides internal peace in our own personal lives. Most of the verses that speak of personal peace in the New Testament refer to peace with God. The lack of this peace is the constant agitation of every lost sinner, as stated in Isaiah 57:20-21: *"the wicked are like the tossing sea, for it cannot be quiet, and its waters toss up mire and dirt. 'There is no peace,' says my God 'for the wicked.'"*

However in Romans 5:1, God tells us how this personal peace is acquired. *"Therefore, having been justified by faith, we have peace with God, through our Lord Jesus Christ."* (NASB)

The promise of salvation, this *"peace with God,"* is provided in Christ Jesus alone:

> For he himself is our peace, who has made us both one and has broken down in his flesh the dividing wall of hostility by abolishing the law of commandments and ordinances, …and might reconcile us both to God in one body through the cross, thereby killing the hostility. And he came and preached peace to you who were far off and peace to those who were near. For through Him we both have access in one Spirit to the Father. (Ephesians 2:14-18)

The comfort of internal peace with God, the Judge is found only through Christ our sole Mediator. Without Him, there never will be peace. *"For there is one God, and there is one Mediator between God and men, the Man Christ Jesus."* (1 Timothy 2:5)

Finally, prayer promotes peace in the church leading believers to exemplify reverential godliness toward God and man.

"so that we may lead a peaceable and quiet life in all godliness and reverence" (1 Tim.2:2)

We may lead: (διαγωμεν) – lead or conduct (αγω-I go, δια-through). This action pictures personal leadership by example as we go through our life. Internal peace with God will cause us to model His peace in our personal relationships in our homes and in the church.

Godliness: (ευσεβεια) – piety, reverence, godliness (God honoring reverence). First and foremost we must model God's peace in such a way that He is reverenced and honored in what we do. Honoring God, then we are enabled to honor men more appropriately.

Reverence / Honesty: (σεμνοτητι) – gravity (man honoring reverence).

This word is used of the children of qualified pastors and deacons in 1 Timothy 3:4, "*One who rules his own house well, having his children in submission with all reverence*." (NKJV) It again addresses the behavior of the students and young adults in Titus 2:6-7: "*Likewise exhort the young men to be sober-minded, in all things showing yourself to be a pattern of good works; in doctrine showing integrity, reverence, incorruptibility, sound speech that cannot be condemned, that one who is an opponent may be ashamed, having nothing evil to say of you*." (NKJV)

These passages reveal that peace in the home, Church, and society is modeled and maintained though loving leadership, and the submissive, respectful attitude of those under authority. This attitude of humble respect which we are all to demonstrate to one another is required by God and is a means of our peace. "*Be kindly affectionate to one another with brotherly love, in honor giving preference to one another*." (Romans 12:10 NKJV)

As we have already seen regarding the external peace of the church, this internal peace provided in the providence and grace of God through prayer and demonstrated in the lives of His people, is a powerful, God-given means of opportunity for the gospel and the discipling of the nations. **This pattern is consistent in Scripture: the peace of the church is designed and provided by God for the evangelizing of the nations.** Note especially the words of Christ: *"I do not ask for these only, but also for those who will believe in me through their word, **that they may all be one**, just as you, Father, are in me, and I in you, that they also may be in us, **so that the world may believe** that you have sent me."* (John 17:20-21, emphasis added) *"By this will all men know that you are my disciples by the love you have one for another."* (John 13:35)

Does your life exemplify prayer and respect toward God and men? Is your life characterized by internal and external peace through prayer – prayer not just for yourself, or even your friends, but especially for *"all who are in authority"* at home, on the road, at school, in the workplace, at church, etc? Do you pray, especially for those who hurt you? Are you in *"one accord"* with others within the body of Christ? Is there peace in your relationships through your peace with God and commitment to intercessory prayer? Have you embraced prayer as an answer to your discord and conflicts in every area of your life? Or are your life and relationships like the troubled sea that has no peace, because you have never bowed in submission to Jesus Christ as your Prince of Peace?

Endnotes

81 Daniel 1:7, 8, 9, 10, 11, 18 speak of the "*Master of the Eunuchs*" under whose authority Daniel and his three friends found themselves, giving evidence that they must have been made eunuchs. In addition, a weak argument from silence can be made in that Daniel and his friends would have obeyed the command to marry in Jeremiah 29:6 if they had not been eunuchs.

82 Charles Ellicott, *The Pastoral Epistles of St. Paul: with a Critical and Grammatical Commentary and a revised Translation* (London: Longmans, Green & Co., 1883), Introduction, xx. Ellicott gives the suggested date of A.D. 66-67. Otis W. Yates, *A Good Soldier of Jesus Christ, An Interpretation of 1 Timothy* (Kansas City, Kansas: Central Seminary Press, 1946), 10. Yates says, "Scholars have virtually agreed that 1 Timothy was written in the summer of A.D. 67". Kenneth S. Wuest, *The Pastoral Epistles in the Greek New Testament*, (Grand Rapids, Michigan: Wm.B. Eerdmans Publishing, 1956), Introduction p.1. Russell Bradley Jones, *The Epistles of First Timothy* (Grand Rapids, Michigan: Baker Book House, 1959), 20. Homes Rolston, *The Layman's Bible Commentary, Thessalonians, Timothy, Titus, Philemon,* (Richmond, Virgina: John Knox Press, 1963), 54. Rolston states: "There is general agreement that the date of composition was about A.D. 65 to 67." Paul F. Barakman, *The Epistles to Timothy and Titus* (Grand Rapids, Michigan: Baker Book House, 1962), 29.

83 Philip Schaff, *History of the Christian Church*, vol. 1, (Grand Rapids: Michigan, Wm. B. Eerdmans Publishing Company, 1910), 379-382.

84 I Timothy 1:3.

85 Marcus Dods and Alexander Whyte, eds., *Handbooks for Bible Classes and Private Students, Pastoral Epistles* by J. P. Lilley (Edinburgh: T. & T. Clark, 1901), 11.

86 Ronald Cox, *It is Paul Who Writes* (New York, NY: Sheed and Ward, 1944), 463.

87 W.E. Vine, Merrill F. Unger, and William White, Jr., *Vine's Complete Expository Dictionary of Old and New Testament Words,* (Nashville, Thomas Nelson Publishers, 1996), 503.

88 *Apology,* XXX, XXXI, XXXII; *The Ante-Nicene Fathers* (Grand Rapids: Eerdmans, reprint 1973), 3:42-43.

89 Theophilus to Autolycus, III.xiv; *The Ante-Nicene Fathers* (Grand Rapids: Eerdmans, reprint 1971), 2:92.

90 Theophilus to Autolycus, III.xiv; *The Ante-Nicene Fathers* (Grand Rapids: Eerdmans, reprint 1971), 2:115.

91 John Calvin, *Institutes of the Christian Religion*, Tran. Henry Beveridge (Grand Rapids, Michigan: Wm. B. Eerdmans Publishing Company, reprint 1998), 664-65.

92 W.E. Vine, Merrill F. Unger, and William White, Jr., *Vine's Complete Expository Dictionary of Old and New Testament Words* (Nashville, Thomas Nelson Publishers, 1996), 503.

It was with this emphasis and vision of the Kingdom Commission in their mind, the early church won the known world in their lifetime.

———————————

True worship of God in obedience to His Word is the heart of missions in leading others to worship the same God we love and serve.

———————————

4

THE PASSION OF GOD: THE ADVANCEMENT OF HIS KINGDOM

*The salvation of political leaders
and religious freedom to spread the gospel*

*Therefore I exhort first of all that supplications, prayers,
intercessions, and giving of thanks be made for all men,
for kings and all who are in authority, that we may lead
a quiet and peaceable life in all godliness and reverence.
For this is good and acceptable in the sight of God our
Savior, who desires all men to be **saved** and to **come to
the knowledge of the truth**.* 1 Timothy 2:1-4 NKJV

In Paul's exhortation to prayer especially for leaders, we find God's express purpose motivating the prayers of His people – the salvation and discipling of the nations. The peace of the Church is a secondary benefit of prayer for all men that focuses on leaders. The ultimate purpose and eternal benefit that God reveals here is His passion for the salvation and discipleship of the nations.

These final two verses form the foundation of this entire passage, commissioning the Church with her responsibility in prayer and ministry of the Word for the salvation of all classes of men, especially kings and all those in authority. The expressed will of God our Savior here communicated to the Church – that all the nations (all men) be saved and come to the knowledge of the truth – is the reason why Christ left heaven and came to die for our sins. This passion of God leaves us with no other option than to pray and minister His Word so that they receive the full benefit God's love portrayed upon the cross.

This Kingdom Commission, *"I exhort first of all that supplications, prayers, intercessions …be made for all men, for kings and all who are in authority"*, includes the will of *"God our Savior, who desires all men to be saved and come to the knowledge of the truth"* and parallels the commission of Matthew 28:19-20 to *"disciple all the nations… teaching them to observe all things that I have commanded you."* This Kingdom Commission is the Great Commission of Acts 1:8, *"You shall be witnesses to Me in Jerusalem, and in all Judea and Samaria, and to the end of the earth"* and Paul's missionary commission of Acts 9:15, *"to bear My name before Gentiles, kings, and the children of Israel."* It was with this emphasis and vision of the Kingdom Commission in their mind, the early church won the known world in their lifetime.

As quoted earlier in Chapter 1 regarding the inexhaustible activity and divinely-blessed success of the

Early Church, and the wildfire spread of the gospel, Albert Barnes states:

> "Within the space *thirty years* after the death of Christ the gospel had been carried to all parts of the civilized and to no small portion of the uncivilized world. Its progress and its triumphs were not concealed. Its great transactions were not "done in a corner." It had assailed the most mighty existing institutions; it had made its way over the most formidable barriers; it had encountered the most deadly and malignant opposition; it had travelled to the capital, and had secured such a hold even in the imperial city as to make it certain that it would finally overturn the established religion and seat itself on the ruins of paganism. Within thirty years it had settled the point that it would overturn every bloody altar, close every pagan temple, bring under its influence everywhere the men of office, rank, and power, and that 'the banners of faith would soon stream from the palace of the Caesars.'"[93]

Having seen the organic and essential unity of the commissions and the power of God that accompanies obedience to this Kingdom Commission, it only remains that we now embrace it as God's method and means of seeing His name worshiped among all the nations. To this end, the Holy Spirit sets before us the beauty of His plan, describing these means as "*good and acceptable*", just as He did at the very beginning, using the same word "*good*" to continually describe His creation.

I. Prayer for leaders and kingdom advancement is essentially good, because it is based on His nature as God our Savior.

In the phrase that begins verse three, "*this is good*" the word "*good*" means intrinsically good, appropriately good, good of itself, right, beautiful, noble and honorable.[94]

WHY IS PRAYER FOR LEADERS ESSENTIALLY GOOD?

First, because it is an act of reliance on the nature of God as Savior. It reveals a dependence on the fullness His attributes, especially His omnipotence and sovereignty in the salvation of men. It proves that we believe in His transforming power when He says, "*The king's heart is like channels of water in the hand of the Lord; He turns it wherever He wishes*" (Proverbs 21:1 NASB).

Prayer proves that we trust in His promise when He says, "*Call to Me, and I will answer you, and show you great and mighty things, which you do not know*" (Jeremiah 33:3 NKJV).

Prayer proves that we believe He is our Father with lavish loving-kindness when He says, "*Ask, and it will be given to you; seek and you will find, knock and it will be opened to you. For everyone who asks receives, and the one who seeks finds, and to the one who knocks it will be opened. Or which one of you, if his son asks him for bread, will give him a stone? Or if he asks for a fish, will give him a serpent?*"

If you then, who are evil, know how to give good gifts to your children, how much more will your Father who is in heaven give good things to those who ask Him?" (Matthew 7:7-11)

Prayer for our leaders and repentant national prayer demonstrates that we have begun to embrace our motto, "IN GOD WE TRUST." Such strategic prayer proves that we trust Him alone to change the course of our nation, praying according to the principle of the promise to Israel, *"If my people, who are called by my name humble themselves, and pray and seek my face and turn from their wicked ways, then I will hear from heaven and will forgive their sin and heal their land"* (2 Chronicles 7:14). According to the principle of this passage, God lays the responsibility of humble, earnest, repentant prayer at the feet of His people for the spiritual health of any nation.

Prayer shows we have embraced the perspective and passion of Christ: *"As You sent Me into the world, so I have also sent them into the world . . . I do not ask for these only, but also for those who will believe in Me through their word"* (John 17:18, 20). Prayer for the salvation of others, requesting that Christ would grant them a complete knowledge of Himself must be the first step in evangelizing them.

Do we believe that God can and will save our political leaders, especially those who oppose Him and His people? When we feel impotent to change the encroaching darkness of our culture, led by those in authority, do we choose to trust God in confident prayer?

Secondly, prayer especially for anti-Christian leaders is essentially good because it is a reflection of the nature of God our Savior, who loves His enemies.

The beauty of an attitude or response which God calls perfect, is especially seen in our love and prayers for those (especially political leaders) who seek our humiliation and destruction. Because we are His children, we reflect the nature of our Father. Jesus shows us how to mirror the love of God in Matthew 5:43-48, particularly as children reflecting their Father. "*But I say to you, 'Love your enemies, and **pray** for those who persecute you, that you may be **sons of your Father who is in heaven**; for He makes His sun rise on the evil and on the good, and sends rain on the just and on the unjust. ... You therefore must be perfect, **as your heavenly Father** is perfect.*'"

There is no greater model than that of Christ on the cross, whose dying prayer was for the forgiveness of his enemies. Jesus received the immediate divine response in the salvation of the very centurion in charge of His crucifixion. As His children, we reflect the work of Christ Himself when we love the lost world, especially our enemies, by praying for the salvation of even those who persecute us.

This is how we perfectly reflect the heart of Christ and our Father, and how we most effectively win to Christ our leaders, our family members, and those around us (especially those who are antagonistic to us and our gospel). And most importantly, this is how we most clearly mirror

"God our Savior, who desires all men to be saved and to come to the knowledge of the truth."

Thirdly, kingdom prayer is essentially good because it displays the worship of an adoring heart for God our Savior in the midst of any circumstance.

The specific **content** of prayer, *"giving of thanks"*, here expresses the joy of a grateful heart in God our Savior. Inherent in this privilege of approaching the King of Kings and Lord of Lords is the appreciation for the privilege He allows us of access: *"supplications"* (the opportunity to enter the throne room of the king to present our petitions), *"prayers"* (a word which speaks exclusively of the privilege of entering the presence of the God of the universe), and *"intercessions"* (the privilege of entering the throne room of the king on behalf of those we love). All of this wonderful privilege elicits a grateful response. However, no access and no rejoicing would be possible were it not for *"God our Savior"*.

Consider the grateful prayers of Paul and Silas. What an example of prevailing prayer in difficult circumstances, resulting even in the salvation of the government official who had executed their suffering! *"About midnight Paul and Silas were **praying** and **singing hymns** to God"* after they had been unlawfully beaten and thrown in the dungeon, with their feet fastened in stocks (Acts 16:24-25). Following their prayers and thanksgiving to God, their Savior, in the hearing of all the prisoners, an earthquake brought the governmental official to his knees imploring Paul and Silas, *"What must I do to be saved?"* (Acts 16:30). True worship of God in obedience to His Word is the heart of missions in leading others to worship the same God we love and serve.

II. Prayer especially for leaders and kingdom advancement is essentially good, because it is His passion to disciple all the nations in truth.

Christ's passion includes all people and especially leaders.

Ponder carefully as to how in the first mention, the Holy Spirit is defining the use of *"all men"* in I Timothy 2. As a part of this Kingdom Commission, the first *"all men"* and those to follow, specifically include an emphasis on *"kings and all who are in authority"* (2:1-2). Because we are prone to overlook or ignore our political leaders (as would be expected of the persecuted believers of Paul's day), Paul continues to emphasize the *"all"*[95] to remind them to include every one of their leaders in verses 1, 2, 4, and 6. In reality, this passage exhorts us to pray for leaders with a triple emphasis (all men, kings, all in authority). Knowing human nature, believers in that day (just as today) would likely have been reluctant to pray for their politicians, especially if they were the source of their persecution. So the *"all men"* in each of these four verses was written to establish in their minds that every group of people was to be included in their prayers and ministry of the Word, especially the authorities, even those who were destroying them. They could be confident also in the salvation of their leaders, because their prayers and witness to them were according to the will of "*God our Savior who desires **all men** to be saved* [emphasizing the inclusion of kings and those in authority]" (v. 4).

Paul, the writer of this letter, was living proof that God demonstrates salvation and great grace even toward those leaders who would persecute the church, making him "*an example for those who would believe in Him for eternal life.*" (1 Tim.1:16 NASB) The fourth "*all*" in verse six is given to further encourage our persistent prayers and bold witness: "*For there is one God and there is one mediator between God and men, the Man Christ Jesus, who gave Himself a ransom for **all**, which is the testimony given at the proper time*" (1 Tim.2:5-6) Prayer in His name and salvation through the only mediator, Jesus Christ, is the absolutely vital priority (Jn.14:6). But the Church must share the gospel with "*all*", even those over them, because the success of the gospel in the lives even of those in authority in every nation around the world has already been assured. **Their ransom has already been paid, we know there are leaders who will believe!**

As Christ said to a disheartened Paul at Corinth, "*Be not afraid, but speak, and do not keep silent; For I am with you, and no one will attack you to hurt you; for I have many people in this city."* As a result of Paul's prayers and ministry of the Word, *"Crispus, the ruler of the synagogue, believed on the Lord with all his household; and many of the Corinthians, hearing, believed, and were baptized."* (Acts 18:10, 8 NKJV) Paul continued there a year and a half and built a flourishing church in probably the most disreputable capital in the empire, and Gallio, the proconsul, refused to allow the Jews to persecute him (Acts 18:12-17) in fulfillment of Christ's promise.

Christ's will and work secures the salvation of "all kinds of people" including leaders.

This statement is the strongest in all of Scripture regarding the will of God in the salvation of men. God is *"willing"* for *"all to be saved."* The verb for *"willing"* (θελω) means "to will, be willing, wish, desire."[96] God delights in the salvation of the lost. His will is accomplished when people are brought to Christ. Literally translated, this passage says: *"God our Savior, all men He wills to be saved and to come to a full knowledge of the truth."* *"To be saved"* is passive, indicating that men are the recipients of His action of salvation. He is the initial, effective, and complete cause in salvation. Only God can do this transforming work in the heart.

How important it is, then, to seek His face in intercession for others, especially for *"kings and all who are in authority".* God loves them more than we do, and He is the source of the exhortation to pray, as well as the efficient cause in answer to our prayers. What a delight to know it is His passion to answer our prayers when we ask for the salvation of others, particularly leaders, according to His perfect will. "*And this is the confidence that we have toward Him, that if we ask anything according to His will He hears us. And if we know that He hears us in whatever we ask, we know that we have the requests that we have asked of Him*" (I John 5:14-15).

Since God has sovereignly chosen to accomplish what He has already declared He would do, and He promises to answer the requests of His people praying according to His will, then we can rest assured that when we pray, His answer is on the way. "*The effective prayer of a righteous man can accomplish much*" (James 5:16 NASB). For our own peace and the sake of our nation, dare we "*sin against the Lord*" by "*ceasing to pray*" (I Samuel 12:23) for our nation and our leaders?

Christ's purpose is the discipleship of all the Nations.

"*For such [praying] is good and right, and [it is] pleasing and acceptable to God our Savior, Who wishes all men to be saved and increasingly to perceive and recognize and discern and know precisely and correctly the [divine] Truth*" (1 Timothy 2:3-4, Amplified Bible).

The pregnant word which the translator emphasizes here in the Amplified Version is the verb "to know" (επιγινωσκω): "*increasingly to perceive and recognize and discern and know precisely and correctly*". This word speaks of a full, advanced knowledge with stress on participation in the truth. This knowledge is "a knowledge which perfectly unites the subject with the object."[97] So this full knowledge of the truth not only refers to salvation, but also discipleship and equipping for ministry. Thus, the root word for salvation (σωζω) being repeated twice, in addition to this word of full knowledge of the truth, combine in a three-fold emphasis on their salvation. This reflects the emphasis of the entire New Testament on God's good nature and volition in choosing the salvation and sanctification of men, providing the final climax to the Kingdom Commissions. God's goodness and passion for the lost are powerfully presented in this context with an undisputable emphasis on grateful prayer for leaders, revealing that we must intentionally fulfill His passion by praying for our authorities and discipling them.

God's passion must be our passion. God's purpose must be our purpose. As another commentator on this passage has said: "God is called 'our Savior' to intimate immediately the claim He has on us, and to indicate the motive we have to pray for the salvation of others, because He saved us. ...any prayer which is good and acceptable in the sight of God is answered prayer. Such prayer springs from a good motive; and is directed toward a good end, because it is a divinely commanded duty as well as a privilege."[98]

Endnotes

93 Robert Frew, ed., *Notes on the New Testament, Explanatory and Practical, Acts,* by Albert Barnes (Grand Rapids, Michigan: Baker Book House, 1980), vii.

94 Ibid, 274.

95 The "*all men*" cannot mean all men without exception (universalism) but instead all men without distinction between Jew and Gentile. It is the compilation of the groups presented in Christ's Commissions, "*all the nations,*" "*Jerusalem, Judea, Samaria, the end of the earth* (Rome)," "*Gentiles, kings, and the children of Israel,*" "*kings and all who are in authority.*"

96 G. Abbott-Smith, *A Manual Greek Lexicon of the New Testament, 3rd Edition* (Edinburgh: U.K., T & T Clark Ltd., 1994), 204.

97 Vine, 347.

98 Otis W. Yates, *A Good Soldier of Christ Jesus, An Interpretation of 1 Timothy* (Kansas City, Kansas: Central Seminary Press, 1946), 51.

The loss of confidence in prayer and the gospel is followed by a loss of the message of the gospel, and results in a loss of the power of the gospel.

CONCLUSION:

The True Hope of the Church

The hope of the church is found in the power of the gospel, preceded and accompanied by fervent prayer. These are the means that God has promised to bless, and has proven to bless throughout the history of the church. Our prayers and evangelism can make a difference in our day just as it did in the First Great Awakening. Jonathan Edwards' description of the America of his day is much like today:

"How lamentable is the moral and religious state of these American colonies! Of New England in particular! How much is that kind of religion which was professed, much experience, and practice, in the first and apparently best times in New England, grown and growing out of credit! What fierce and violent contentions have been of late among ministers and people, about things of a religious nature! How much is the Gospel ministry grown into contempt! And the work of the ministry, in many respects, laid under uncommon difficulties, and even in danger of sinking amongst us! How many of our congregations and churches rending in pieces!

Church discipline weakened, and ordinances less and less regarded! What wild and extravagant notions, gross delusions of the devil, and strange practices have prevailed, and still do prevail in many places, under a pretext of extraordinary purity, spirituality, liberty, and zeal against formality, usurpation, and conformity to the world! How strong and deeply rooted, and general are the prejudices that prevail against vital religion and the power of godliness, and almost everything that pertains to it, or tends to it! How apparently are the hearts of people, everywhere, uncommonly shut up against all means and endeavors to awaken sinners and revive religion! Vice and immorality, of all kinds, withal increasing and unusually prevailing! …never was there an age, wherein religion in general was so much despised and trampled on, and Jesus Christ and God Almighty blasphemed and treated with open, daring contempt."[99]

The times had become so bad on both sides of the ocean that 12 pastors in Scotland met together in October of 1744 and agreed to pray and led their people to pray for two years, especially on Saturday evening and Sunday morning and "more solemnly on the first Tuesday of each quarter, beginning the first Tuesday of November."[100] They sent about 500 invitations (called a "Memorial") to a pastor in Boston who sent them to pastors throughout the American Colonies to join them in prayer for 7 years. Edwards received his "Memorial" and responded with a treatise on prayer to encourage all the Christians throughout the colonies to join in prayer in response to the invitation of the Scottish pastors. They all agreed and made prayer their priority (and that commitment seems to have continued on the part of the American Church until at least 1825).

The result was the First Great Awakening. God not only transformed literally thousands of hearts in America for Christ, but granted this country a radical change in morality, charity and even Government. God's mercy in answer to prayer was so abundant that even modern, secular historians recognize, "By 1815 America had become the most evangelically Christian nation in the world."[101]

Why do our elections take place on the first Tuesday in November? That day seems to have been a celebration of the **first day of prayer** when the churches united together and prayed in 1746. God eventually answered in such a way that the nation grew to be one which depended upon God. And today, "In God We Trust" must be more than our motto. It must speak of our complete dependence upon God in prayer, first as individuals, then as churches and communities of churches. Perhaps God in mercy will grant us an awakening again, not only in our nation, but around the world!

God has already begun answering the prayers of His people across this nation in many ways. The Congressional Prayer Caucus website provides some exciting recent history:

"In 2005, Congressman J. Randy Forbes gathered a small group of members of the U.S. House of Representatives who began meeting in Room 219 of the Capital to pray for our nation. These Members later formed The Congressional Prayer Caucus – an official Caucus of the U.S. House of Representatives – to formally acknowledge the important role that prayer plays in American life and history and to monitor and work to guard the right of individuals in America to pray. Currently, Congressman Forbes and Congressman Mike McIntyre serve as the co-chairmen of this Caucus. Today, the Prayer Caucus has grown to a bipartisan group of 100 Members dedicated to protecting religious liberty and recognizing our nations' rich, spiritual history."[102]

May God encourage you to commit to daily prayer for your leaders. God delights to hear you pray in faith, and ask for those things that only He can do! He promises in Jeremiah 33:3, *"Call to Me, and I will answer you and show you great and mighty things which you do not know."* (NKJV) Shall we not commit to our government leaders as Samuel did to his king before all the people on his Coronation Day in I Samuel 12:23-24, *"Moreover, as for me, far be it from me that I should sin against the LORD by ceasing to pray for you, and I will instruct you in the good and the right way. Only fear the LORD, and serve him faithfully with all your heart: for consider what great things he has done for you."*

Specific ways to apply the priority of prayer and ministry of the Word to our leaders:

1) When giving thanks for your meals, remember your leaders.

2) When praying publicly in church meetings, remember your leaders by name.

3) When praying privately, remember your leaders by name.

4) Every April 6, the day Christ witnessed a good confession before Pilate,[103] set aside the day possibly for fasting and particularly for prayer for your nation's leaders, corporately or individually. This would be a G.L.A.D. way to intercede and give thanks for our leaders.

   G lobal

   L eadership

   A ppreciation

   D ay of Prayer

5) Consider sending notes to your leaders, letting them know you are praying for them, particularly on their birthday (the day a note will be best received).

6) Minister the Word to your leaders through a personal visit to your state and federal legislators.

7) Develop a strategy for you and your church to disciple your community, your city, your state, your nation and particularly "*all the nations*" (Mt. 28:19-20).

8) Take the first step to "*disciple all the nations*" by acquiring a "World Prayer Map" detailing the countries of the world, their population, their President, and the percentage of believers, to pray for them. Call 800-423-5054 or order online at www.EHC.org.

9) Sign up to receive daily updates by email to pray for the government leaders of your state and the nation at www.pray1tim2.org or visit our website at www. capitolcom.org to see the respective states where you can acquire a prayer list of your leaders and pray for us in our respective states ministering to our leaders. Also, consider partnering with us in this strategic ministry.

This specific means and method of discipling leaders is precisely the goal and ministry of Capitol Commission. We are "Reaching Capitol Communities for Christ" and bringing the Great Commission to the leaders of our state, our nation and the world. Not only have we provided leadership prayer lists in states where we have a ministry in order to effectively obey 1 Timothy 2:1-4, but a daily prayer reminder for each individual State can be received by email, registering at www.pray1tim2.org. In addition, we seek to win and disciple our leaders through Bible studies in the Capitol, distributing expositional Bible study notes, thereby providing our leaders access to the "*full knowledge of the truth.*" Both the prayer lists and Bible studies are found on our website at www.capitolcom.org.

We close this book praying with George Washington for the peace and prosperity of the United States of America:

Almighty God, we make our earnest prayer that Thou wilt keep the United States in thy holy protection, that Thou wilt incline the hearts of the citizens to cultivate a spirit of subordination and obedience to government and entertain a brotherly affection and love for one another and for their fellow citizens of the United States at large,

And finally that Thou wilt most graciously be pleased to dispose us all to do justice, to love mercy, and to demean ourselves with that charity, humility and pacific temper of mind which were the characteristics of the Divine Author of our blessed religion, and without an humble imitation of whose example in these things, we can never hope to be a happy nation.

Grant our supplications, we beseech Thee, through Jesus Christ our Lord. Amen. (Written at Newburg, June 8, 1783, and sent to the Governors of all the States.)[104]

Heavenly Father,

We rejoice that You are The King over all and You have invited us before Your throne with those wonderful promises in Jesus Christ, "*Ask, and it will be given to you; seek, and you will find; knock, and it will be opened to you: For everyone who asks receives, and he who seeks finds, and to the one who knocks it will be opened.*" As Your people we ask that You might pour out your saving grace upon our leaders. May they know by experience the joy of Your loving sovereignty as Lord. We ask for our President, our Vice President, for each one in the Cabinet, the Congress, and the Supreme Court that You might transform each of their hearts and graciously gather them into Your Kingdom.

May they delight themselves in You and find that You give them the desire of their heart. We ask the same for our own State leaders, our Governor, our Lt. Governor, our Attorney General, the Speaker of the House, and each one in the Cabinet, the Senate, the House of Delegates and our Supreme Court, may not one of them escape Your grace. We ask that You move in their hearts and ours to call upon Your Name, that we all may humble ourselves and pray and seek Your face and turn from our wicked ways that we may hear from heaven and find forgiveness for our sin and healing for our land.

Please forgive us for our lack of prayer and teach us to pray, according to our first priority found in 1 Tim. 2:1-4, and help us to especially pray for our leaders. Please grant us a revival of prayer that begins with us and spreads throughout our nation and to the nations beyond.

Oh Father, we long for Your Kingdom to come to our own hearts, and especially in the hearts of our leaders. You tell us in Proverbs 21:1 that *"The king's heart is like channels of water in the hand of the Lord; He turns it wherever He wishes."* May You turn the hearts of our leaders to You. Please help us to especially pray for our pastors.

We ask that You may start a revival of prayer among our pastors and our churches, so that You may have mercy upon our land. We thank You for that promise given to Jeremiah in the darkest hour, *"Call to Me, and I will answer you and show you great and mighty things which you do not know."*

May You show us those great and mighty things in answer to our prayer. May You grant to each of us as Your people a delight in prayer and in Your Word. We ask these things in the all sufficient name of Jesus Christ, our Savior, Amen.

Endnotes

99 Jonathan Edwards, *The Works of Jonathan Edwards*, vol. 2 (Avon, England: The Bath Press, reprint The Banner of Truth Trust, 1992), 293.

100 Ibid, 283.

101 Gordon S. Wood, *Empire of Liberty: A History of the Early Republic, 1789-1803, The Oxford History of the United States* (New York: Oxford University Press, 2009), 3.

102 Congressional Prayer Caucus, http://forbes.house.gov/Prayer Caucus/About.aspx (accessed January 18, 2014).

103 The precise date, April 6, 30 AD is from James Montgomery Boice, *The Gospel of Matthew*, vol. 1, *The King and His Kingdom , Matthew 1-17* (Grand Rapids, Michigan: Baker Books, 2001), 219-223.

104 Ivan L. Bennett, Ed., *Song and Service Book for Ship and Field Army and Navy* (New York, New York: A.S. Barnes and Company, Inc., 1942), front flyleaf.

Appendix 1

On National Prayer for Revival
by Jonathan Edwards [105]

A Humble Attempt to Promote the Agreement and Union of God's People Throughout the World in Extraordinary Prayer For a Revival Of Religion And The Advancement Of God's Kingdom On Earth, According To Scriptural Promises And Prophecies Of The Last Time.

The Future Glorious State of Christ's Church

"This is what the LORD Almighty says: 'Many peoples and the inhabitants of many cities will yet come, and the inhabitants of one city will go to another and say, 'Let us go at once to entreat the LORD and seek the LORD Almighty. I myself am going.' And many peoples and powerful nations will come to Jerusalem to seek the LORD Almighty and to entreat him" (Zechariah 8:20-22).

In this chapter Zechariah prophecies of the future, glorious advancement of the Church. It is evident there is more intended than was ever fulfilled in the Jewish nation during Old Testament times. Here are plain prophecies describing things that were never fulfilled before the coming of Messiah, particularly what is said in the two last verses in the chapter where Zechariah speaks of 'many people and strong nations worshiping and seeking the true God,' and of so great an addition of Gentiles to the Church that the majority of visible worshipers consist of Gentiles, outnumbering the Jews ten to one.

Nothing ever happened, from the time of Zechariah to the coming of Christ, to fulfill this prophecy. Its fulfillment can only be in the calling of the Gentiles during and following apostolic times, or in the future, glorious enlargement of God's Church in the end times, so often foretold by Old Testament prophets, particularly by Zechariah. It is most likely that the Spirit of God speaks here of the greatest revival and the most glorious advancement of the Church on earth, the blessings of which will benefit the Jewish nation.

Indeed, there is great agreement on this point, between this prophecy of Zechariah, and other prophecies concerning the Church's latter day glory. Consider Isaiah 60:2-4,

> 'See, darkness covers the earth and thick darkness is over the peoples, but the Lord rises upon you and his glory appears over you. Nations will come to your light, and kings to the brightness of your dawn. Lift up your eyes and look about you: All assemble and come to you; your sons come from afar, and your daughters are carried on the arm.'

Without doubt, this entire chapter foretells the most glorious state of the God's Church on earth, as does Isaiah 66:8, Micah 4:1-3 and Isaiah 2:1-4:

'In the last days the mountain of the LORD'S temple will be established as chief among the mountains; it will be raised above the hills, and peoples will stream to it.'

'Many nations will come and say, 'Come, let us go up to the mountain of the LORD, to the house of the God of Jacob. He will teach us his ways, so that we may walk in his paths.'

'The law will go out from Zion, the word of the LORD from Jerusalem. He will judge between many peoples and will settle disputes for strong nations far and wide. They will beat their swords into plowshares and their spears into pruning hooks. Nation will not take up sword against nation, nor will they train for war anymore.'

Nothing whatsoever has happened to fulfill these prophecies. Moreover, since the prophecy in my text (Zech. 8:20-22) and the following verse agrees with them, there is reason to think it addresses the same times. Indeed, there is remarkable agreement in the description given throughout this chapter with the representations of those times elsewhere in the prophetic books.

Though the prophet is at times referring to the future smiles of heaven on the Jewish nation, yet the Spirit of God doubtlessly refers to events far greater than these, of which these are but faint resemblances. The Jews had just returned from the Babylonian captivity, Chaldea and other countries, and resettled in Canaan where they were experiencing great increase of both numbers and wealth.

We find it common in the prophecies of the Old Testament that when the prophets are speaking of the favors and blessings of God on the Jews, attending or following their return from the Babylonian captivity, the Spirit of God takes the opportunity from there to speak of the incomparably greater blessings on the Church, that will attend and follow her deliverance from the spiritual Babylon, of which those were a type.

The prophet, in this chapter, speaks of God's bringing his people again from the east and west to Jerusalem (vs. 7-8), and multitudes of all nations taking hold of the skirts of the Jews. Although this prophecy literally refers to the Jews return from Babylon, its fulfillment cannot be seen there for no such things spoken of here attended their return. Therefore, it must refer to the great calling and gathering of Jews into the fold of Christ, and to them receiving the blessings of His kingdom, after the fall of the Antichrist and the destruction of the spiritual Babylon.

THE POWER OF PRAYER

In Zechariah 8:20-22 we have an account of how this future advancement of the Church should occur. It would come to fruition as multitudes from different towns resolve to unite in extraordinary prayer, seeking God until He manifests Himself and grants the fruits of his presence. We may observe several things in particular:

1. THE NECESSITY OF PRAYER.

Some suppose that prayer includes the whole of worship to God and that prayer is a part of worship during the days of the gospel when sacrifices are abolished. Therefore, this can be understood as a prophecy of a great revival of religion with true worship of God among His people, repentance from idolatry, and growth of the Church.

However, it seems reasonable to me to suppose that something even more special is intended regarding prayer given that prayer is not only repeatedly mentioned, but that this prophecy parallels many other prophecies that speak of an extraordinary spirit of prayer preceding that glorious day of revival and advancement of the Church's peace and prosperity. It particularly parallels what the prophet later speaks of the 'pouring out of a spirit of grace and supplications' as that which introduces the great religious revival (Zech. 12:10).

2. THE GOOD WHICH SHALL BE BROUGHT BY PRAYER: GOD HIMSELF.

Scripture says, 'They shall go to pray before the Lord, and to seek the Lord of Hosts.' The good that they seek for is 'The Lord of Hosts,' Himself. If 'seeking God' means no more than seeking the favor or mercy of God then 'praying before the Lord,' and 'seeking the Lord of Hosts' must be looked upon as synonymous. However, 'seeking the Lord' is commonly used to mean something far more than seeking something from God. Surely it implies that God Himself is what is desired and sought after.

Thus, the Psalmist desired God, thirsted after Him and sought after Him:

'O God, thou art my God; early will I seek thee. My flesh longeth for thee, in a dry and thirsty land, where no water is, to see thy power and thy glory, so as I have seen thee in the sanctuary... My soul followeth hard after thee... Whom have I in heaven by thee? And there is none upon earth that I desire besides thee.'

The Psalmist earnestly pursued after God; his soul thirsted after Him, he stretched forth his hands unto Him. All of God's saints have this in common: they are those that seek God. 'This is the generation of them that seek Him.' 'Your heart shall live that seek God,' etc.

If this be the true sense of this phrase 'seeking the Lord of Hosts,' then we must understand that God who had withdrawn Himself, or, as it were, hid Himself, would return to His Church, granting the fruits of His presence and communion with His people, which He so often promised, and for which His Church had so long waited.

In short, it seems reasonable to understand the phrase, 'seeking the Lord of Hosts' means not merely praying to God, but seeking the promised restoration of the Church of God after the Babylonian captivity and the great apostasy occasioning it is called their 'seeking God, and searching for Him;' and God's granting this promised revival and restoration called His being 'found of them.' (See Jer. 29:10-14)

The prophets occasionally represent God as being withdrawn and hiding Himself: 'Verily thou art a God that hideth thyself, O God of Israel, the Savior. I hid me, and was wroth.' The prophets then go on to represent God's people seeking Him, searching and waiting for and calling after Him. When God answers their prayers and restores and advances His people, according to His promise, then He is said to come and say, 'Here am I' and to show Himself, and they are said to find Him and see Him plainly.

'Then you will call, and the Lord will answer; you will cry for help, and he will say: Here am I...'

'But Israel will be saved by the Lord with an everlasting salvation... I have not said to Jacob's descendants, 'Seek me in vain.' I, the Lord, speak the truth; I declare what is right.'

'The Sovereign Lord will wipe away the tears from all faces; he will remove the disgrace of his people from all the earth. In that day they will say, 'Surely this is our God; we trusted in him, and he saved us. This is the Lord, we trusted in him; let us rejoice and be glad in his salvation.' We wait for you; your name and renown are the desire of our hearts.' (Isa. 58:9; Isa. 45:17,19; Isa. 25:8-9)

3. WE MAY OBSERVE WHO IT IS THAT WILL BE UNITED IN SEEKING THE LORD:

'The inhabitants of many cities... yea, many people and strong nations.' Many people from all over the world will unite to seek the Lord.

From the prophecy, it seems reasonable to assume that this will be fulfilled in the following manner: First, God's people will be given a spirit of prayer, inspiring them to come together and pray in an extraordinary manner, that He would help his Church, show mercy to mankind in general, pour out his Spirit, revive His work, and advance His kingdom in the world as He promised.

Moreover, such prayer would gradually spread and increase more and more, ushering in a revival of religion. This would be characterized by greater worship and service of God among believers. Others will be awakened to their need for God, motivating them to earnestly cry out to God for mercy. They will be led to join with God's people in that extraordinary seeking and serving of God which they see around them. **In this way the revival will grow until the awakening reaches whole nations and those in the highest positions of influence.** The Church will grow to be ten times larger than it was before. Indeed, at length, all the nations of the world will be converted unto God.

Thus, ten men, out of all languages and nations, will 'take hold of the skirt of' the Jew (in the sense of the Apostle), saying 'We will go with you, for we have heard that God is with you.' Thus will be fulfilled, 'O thou that heareth prayer, unto thee shall all flesh come.'

4. WE MAY ALSO OBSERVE THE MANNER OF THEIR UNITY IN PRAYER.

It is a visible and voluntary union that was first proposed by some of God's people with others readily joining in over time. Those who live in one city will declare to those of another city, 'Let us go' etc. Many of those who hear their declaration will not only join with them but will make the call for the unity in prayer known to still others. As a result, the movement will grow, prevail and spread among God's people.

Some suppose that the words, 'I will go also,' are to be taken as words spoken by the one making the proposal. He states this expressing his willingness and desire to do what he is asking his hearer to do. But this is to suppose no more than is expressed in the phrase, 'Come and let us go...' itself. It seems more natural to me to understand these words as being the consent or reply of the one to whom the proposal is made.

This is much more agreeable to the flow of the text which represents the compliance of great numbers of people in this movement. And though if these words are thus understood, we must suppose something understood in the text that is not expressed: Those of other cities will say, 'I will go also.' Yet, this is not difficult to conceive of as such figures of speech are common in the Scripture (Jer. 3:22; Ps. 1:6,7).

5. NEXT, WE CAN OBSERVE THE MANNER IN WHICH THEY AGREE TO PRAY:

'Let us go speedily to pray,' or, as it says in the margin: let us go continually. Literally translated this means, 'let us go in going.' The Hebrew language often doubles words for emphasis (e.g., the holy of holies signifies that which is most holy). Such repetition of words also denotes the certainty of an event coming to pass. For example, when God said to Abraham, 'in multiplying, I will multiply thy seed,' God implies that He would certainly multiply his seed, and multiply it exceedingly.

6. FINALLY, THIS PROPHECY GIVES US A PICTURE OF THIS UNION IN PRAYER BEING AN INVITING AND A HAPPY THING.

We sense God's pleasure, and the results prove tremendously successful. From the whole of this prophecy we may infer that it is well pleasing to God for many people, in different parts of the world, to voluntarily come into a visible union to pray in an extraordinary way for those great outpourings of the Holy Spirit which shall advance the Kingdom of our Lord Jesus Christ that God has so often promised shall be in the latter ages of the world.

An Example From History

Let me relate a brief history of what has happened in Scotland:

In October of 1744, a number of ministers in Scotland, considering the state of God's Church, and mankind in general, believed that God was calling those concerned for the welfare of the Church to unite in extraordinary prayer. They knew God was the Creator and source of all blessings and benefits in the Church so they earnestly prayed that He would appear in His glory, and strengthen the Church, and manifest His compassion to the world of mankind by an abundant outpouring of His Holy Spirit. They desired a true revival in all parts of Christendom, and to see nations delivered from their great and many calamities, and to bless them with the unspeakable benefits of the Kingdom of our glorious Redeemer, and to fill the whole earth with His glory.

These ministers consulted with one another on this subject and concluded that they were obliged to begin such prayer and attempt to persuade others to do the same. After seeking God for direction, they determined that for the next two years they would set apart some time on Saturday evenings and Sunday mornings every week for prayer as one's other duties would allow. More importantly, it was decided that the first Tuesday of each quarter (**beginning with the first Tuesday of November**) would be time to be spent in prayer. People were to pray for either the entire day or part of the day, as they found themselves disposed, or as circumstances allowed. They would meet in either private prayer groups or in public meetings, whichever was found to be most convenient.

It was determined that none should make any promises or feel under strict obligation to observe every one of these days without fail; for these days were not holy or established by sacred authority. However, to prevent negligence, and the temptation to make excuses for trivial reasons, it was proposed that if those who resolve to pray cannot take part on the agreed upon day, they would use the next available day for the purpose of prayer.

The primary reason for this cooperation in prayer was to maintain, among the people of God, that necessity of prayer for the coming of Christ's Kingdom, which Christ directed his followers to do. We are, unfortunately, too little inclined to pray because of our laziness and immaturity, or because of the distraction of our own worldly, private affairs. We have prayed at times, but without special seasons for prayer, we are, likely, to neglect it either partially or totally. But when we set aside certain times for prayer, resolving to fulfill this commission unless extraordinarily hindered, we are less likely to neglect it.

The return of each new season will naturally refresh the memory and will cause us to remember these teachings of our Lord Jesus Christ, and the obligations we have as His followers. We will be renewed in the importance, necessity and unspeakable value of the mercy we seek from God, and by frequent renovation, the vision to pray will be kept alive in our hearts at all times. Therefore, those ministers from Scotland determined that such gatherings would help encourage greater prayerfulness among God's people for revival throughout the year. They also believed that the quarterly gathering would encourage and strengthen people to pray, especially if they knew that many other Christians in so many distant places were praying for the same things at a same time.

It was thought that two years would be a sufficient trial period, after which time would be given to evaluate fruitfulness of the endeavor. It was not known but thought best to allow some time to make some adjustments if necessary. The time period, though short, was thought sufficient to judge its fruitfulness. Those involved would have the opportunity to communicate their thoughts, and perhaps improve, on this manner of prayer.

As for promulgating this concert of prayer, the ministers decided to simply pass the word through personal conversation, and correspondence with others far away, rather than any formal advertisement in the press. At first it was intended that some formal paper outlining the proposal should be sent around for proper amendments and improvements, and then agreement. But after more thoughtful deliberation, it was concluded that this would only give rise to objections which they thought best to avoid in the beginning.

Great success seems to have met their labors for great numbers in Scotland and England, and even some in North America joined with them. As to Scotland, many people in the four chief cities, Edinburgh, Glasgow, Aberdeen, and Dundee joined. There were also many country towns and congregations in various other areas that participated. A Mr. Robe, of Kilsyth, stated that 'There were then above thirty societies of young people there, newly erected, some of which consisted of upwards of thirty members.'

The two years ended last November. Just prior to this, a number of ministers in Scotland agreed on a letter, to be printed and sent abroad to their brethren, proposing to them, and requesting of them, to join with them in continuing this concert of prayer, and in the endeavors to promote it. Almost five hundred copies of this letter were sent over to New England, with instructions to distribute them to the Massachusetts-Bay area, Connecticut, New Hampshire, Rhode Island, New York, New Jersey, Pennsylvania, Maryland, Virginia, Carolina and Georgia. Most were sent to a congregational minister in Boston along with a letter from twelve ministers in Scotland. Other copies were sent to other ministers in Boston, and some to a minister in Connecticut.

The proposal, dated August 26, 1746, opens with an explanation of the purpose and times for the concerts of prayer, and an entreaty to the ministers to communicate their opinions after the two year period had completed.

The ministers then go on to assure their Bostonian brethren that the concerts are not to be seen as binding; men are not expected to set apart days from secular affairs, or 'fix on any part of ... precise days, whether it be convenient or not.' Nor are they to be seen as 'absolute promises, but as friendly, harmonious resolutions, with liberty to alter circumstances as shall be found expedient.' Because of such liberty these prayer times cannot be judged to infringe upon those 'religious times' appointed by men.

The letter also asked ministers to consider composing and publishing short 'persuasive directions' regarding the necessity of prayer, either by particular authors or several joining together. Without such repeated reminders men are apt to become weary and begin to neglect their duty. Ministers are also asked to preach frequently on the importance and necessity of prayer for the coming of the Lord's Kingdom, particularly near or on the quarterly times.

The Boston ministers are to understand that these prayer concerts are not restricted to any particular denomination, but is extended to all who have 'at heart the interest of vital Christianity, and the power of godliness; and who, however differing about other things, are convinced of the importance of fervent prayer...'

It was proposed that the prayer should extend for seven more years and the ministers agreed to this. However there was concern that zeal for spreading news of the concert would wane because of the length proposed. Nevertheless, it was agreed that the first period of time (two years) was too short.

If persons who formerly agreed to this concert should discontinue it, would it not look like that fainting in prayer Scripture so ardently warned against? Would this not be particularly unsuitable given the need of public reformation?

Those ministers in Boston said of this proposal: 'The motion seems to come from above, and to be wonderfully spreading in Scotland, England, Wales, Ireland and North America.'

This is a short online version of the treatise on prayer by Jonathan Edwards and the complete treatise can be found in *The Works of Jonathan Edwards*, Vol. 2, (Edinburgh: Scotland, Banner of Truth Trust, 1992), "VII A Humble Attempt to Promote Explicit Agreement and Visible Union of God's People in Extraordinary Prayer for the Revival of Religion and the Advancement of Christ's Kingdom on Earth," pages 278-311.

Or in singular book form, *Praying Together for True Revival* by Jonathan Edwards, and published by P&R Publishing, presents the treatise in modern English with added study questions. This treatise was the outstanding work that God used to excite the churches of America to prayer through which God Granted the First Great Awakening.

---

105 Grace Online Library, http://www.graceonlinelibrary.org/church-ministry/revival/jonathan-edwards-on-corporate-prayer-for-revival/ (Accessed July 30, 2013).

Appendix 2

A Kingdom Call to Women to Pray for Their Nations' Capitols and Leadership

God's plan has always been to save the nations. John 3:16 tells us *"For God so loved the world that He gave us His Son..."* We know the Scriptures; we know 1 Timothy 2:1-4 tells us all to pray for *"kings and all those in authority"*; we know that Samuel said of the truculent King Saul, *"God forbid that I should sin against God by ceasing to pray for you,"* teaching us that is a sin not to pray for political leadership; we know that David said *"I will speak of thy testimonies also before kings and will not be ashamed"* (Psalm 119:46); and we know that when the Lord Jesus Christ commissioned Saul (Acts 9:15), he told him he would *"bear My name before ...kings,"* to share the gospel with them.

But are these Scriptures speaking just in general terms, or is reaching kings and reaching them in their capitols a vital part of God's plan and strategy to reach the world for Christ? On close inspection it would appear that God's plan and method has always been to target national capitals and national leadership, as well as individuals for Himself and for His Christ. In Revelation 21 there is a description of the New Jerusalem and we find that, *"By its light shall the nations walk and the kings of the earth shall bring their glory into it."*

Recently I listened to David Andersen, Capitol Commission director for the state of Virginia, present a workshop on this very topic at the 2013 Global Conference, "Turn on the Light" in Washington DC (Capitol Commission partnered with Parlamento y Fe of Argentina to host the conference). He proved from the Scriptures that God indeed does have such a plan, and that His strategy is and always has been to target and reach the capitals of the world and world empires for Himself and for His Christ. As I listened I became greatly intrigued and quite excited, as though on the verge of a great discovery. David pointed out that all the Old Testament prophets were raised up by God to speak to the kings of Israel and to world empire leaders in their capitols. He also pointed out that in the New Testament, Christ's strategy was to reach the national leadership, including His final witness to Pontius Pilate. Paul's strategy, too, was to target capital cities with the gospel, establish churches in those cities, ending in Rome, the imperial capital of the Roman Empire. Kings impact their nations, and can impact their nations for God. God holds national leaders accountable for their nation's works and their response to the gospel (Matthew 25:31ff).

I was also to present a workshop during that same week to the women who attended the conference. I was given the topic, "Developing a Ministry to Women in Politics". I had (prayerfully) chosen to include in my message the significant women of the Bible that had impacted national leadership and or legislation. I left David's workshop wondering, is the same pattern demonstrated with the significant women of scripture? Are women included in His plan and strategy to reach capitols? Does God purposely raise up women to *"Speak of thy testimonies also before kings"*? Could those women be the same women on which I had chosen to speak? I could hardly wait to find time to get away to study and think and pray. The next morning as I studied I was excited to find that the same plan and strategy is indeed there in Scripture. God raised up women also to speak to kings and to the national leadership in the capitals of the world to impact each kingdom with His kingdom.

God also led me to Jeremiah 9:17-21, where God directed Jeremiah to *"Call for the wailing women"* to weep, lament, pray, and intercede for the capital city of Jerusalem about to suffer the consequences of turning from God. God also instructed the women to teach their daughters to intercede for their capital city. So I believe we have biblical evidence to support the fact that God is calling women, not only to raise families for Him, but also to have an impact in government; that we women have a mandate from Him to pray for our political leaders, a Kingdom Commission. Let's look at the evidence. And this is not an exhaustive study; this is a bird's eye view of the evidence. Possibly a more extensive study will follow, Lord willing.

The Biblical Evidence

Just as God sent male prophets to speak to kings and national leadership in the capital cities of their nations, so

God has used women, whether they are wives, mothers, widows, sisters, daughters, single women, or working women. There may not be as many but use them He has and does.

The first record of women impacting a nation is the **Hebrew midwives**, a group of nurses, a group of working women, who when told directly by Pharaoh, king of Egypt, to abort all the baby boys of their ethnic group, they disobeyed the king because *"they feared God"* more (Exodus 1:15-22). Through their action they assured the continuation of the children of Israel, God's chosen Kingdom. Had they not, there would have been no nation of Israel, no Moses, no Joshua, and later no David, no kingdom of Israel, and no Messiah, the Lord Jesus Christ. Yes, this is an example of civil disobedience, but it is the example of faith in obeying God rather than man, because the women believed God's promise to their ancestor Abraham of a kingdom through which the Messiah would come (Genesis 12:1-3). James says in his epistle that *"faith"* without *"works is dead"* (James 2:17-18). The Hebrew midwives showed their faith by their works. God used them in the establishment of His kingdom on earth, and recorded their names, Shiphra and Puah, for eternity.

Miriam, the first prophetess mentioned in Scripture (Exodus 2:4-10; 15:1-21; Numbers 12:1-15; 20:1) and sister to Moses, was used by God as a child to save the life of her baby brother Moses, whom God would raise up to become the first leader of that promised nation, Israel. Miriam ministered beside her brother Moses when he was the leader of the nation of Israel. After the victory over Pharaoh's army, she led the women to sing and praise God for the victory. However, as the first prophetess mentioned, she became an example to the women whom God would later raise up. She was not to seek to usurp the authority of God's appointed male leadership, or to criticize or to speak out publicly against them, because when Miriam spoke against Moses God struck her with leprosy, and she later died in the wilderness, denied her life goal of entering the Promised Land. I believe this example gives clear warning to the women whom God calls to pray for capitols and national leadership that we are not to be publicly critical of political leaders, their policy, actions, or their character, and we are not to seek to rally support to undermine their authority.

Deborah the prophetess (Judges 4 and 5) ministered in the southern end of the tribe of Ephraim, the ancestral allotment of Joshua, the great military leader of Israel. The Philistines and Canaanites had overrun the Promised Land and Canaanite King Jabin had made the city of Hazor in Naphtali his capital city again (Joshua 11:10). All God's people lived in oppression and fear. The Bible tells us that the responsibility for the national disaster lay squarely at the feet of the nation's male leadership for not obeying God and completely routing the wicked enemy from the land (Deuteronomy 7:1-6; Judges 2:10-15), though Deborah never said as much. I am sure she was mindful of the example of Miriam because Deborah was never critical of the male leadership in Israel and in her efforts to help never sought to undermine their authority. Instead she says in Judges 5:9 that *"Her heart went out to the rulers of Israel."* She said of herself, "I'm just a mother", but she says she *"arose"* to do something about the problem (Judges 5:7). She rose to national leadership as judge and set up her ministry headquarters centrally between the cities of Ramah and Bethel in the hill country of Ephraim, Judges 4:5. The people needed leadership that would help them in that time of national crisis. By faith she summoned a reluctant Barak from the city of Kedesh-Naphtali, a principal city of the tribe of Naphtali and a City of Refuge (Judges 4:6, Joshua 20:7, 21:32), and said she knew that God was calling him to rally the Israelite tribal leaders to unite and form an army to route the enemy. Barak said he would only go if Deborah went with him. But Deborah stood with Barak and the small army that he mustered, went with them to battle at Mt. Tabor, and God did indeed give them the victory. The land subsequently had peace for forty years.

Hannah was a young mom whose prayer for her nation is recorded in 1 Samuel 2:1-11. This was at a time when the spiritual leadership of Israel was corrupt (1 Samuel 2:12-17), and there was no national unifying leadership. We know that Hannah taught this prophetic prayer to her small son, Samuel, because as the author of the book he says this was his mother's prayer. It is an amazing prayer of praise, full of the theology and prophecy on which the Kingdom of Israel would be built. It proclaims that God is the King and

Judge of the entire earth, and that His kingdom will prevail over the kingdoms of man and evil men, and that He will set up His kingdom on earth. This prayer shaped Samuel's faith and practice when he rose to become Judge of the nation of Israel, and it shaped the way he discipled a young man by the name of David. King David established Jerusalem as the spiritual and political capital of Israel. The Book of Psalms over and over again testifies to David's faith and theology handed down in part from Samuel through a young mom named Hannah. Indeed David's rise to become king is the fruit of Hannah's prayer for her nation. King David is the ancestor of the Messiah, the Lord Jesus Christ, the King and Anointed one of Hannah's prayer.

Abigail (1 Samuel 25) interfered with the determined murderous path of the future king of Israel. Abigail was a wife in a difficult marriage, but we are told that she was beautiful, and "*a woman of good understanding*," meaning that she was sure of her faith and theology. She believed that God had chosen David to be the next king of Israel. Nabal, her husband was a supporter of King Saul. When David's men went to Nabal for payment for their security work of watching Nabal's flocks, he insulted them and David, and sent them away empty handed. David, incensed, armed his men and set off to wipe out Nabal and his whole household in retaliation. When Abigail found out what had happened she set off to meet David to plead with him and prevent disaster. Her petition to David sought to avoid blood on his hands when God brought him to the throne, and it worked. God used Abigail to directly impact the character and reputation of the future king of Israel. It was through her wise intercession that the shepherd king of Israel never harmed one of his own flock.

Huldah, the little known prophetess of 2 Kings 22:23 was the wife of the keeper of the Temple's priestly and or royal robes and lived in the capital city of Jerusalem. God's Book of the Law had been found in the Temple after generations of neglect by the nation's spiritual and political leadership and it proclaimed impending doom on the nation of Israel for its sins. When King Josiah learned of it he became distressed and sent priests to pray and inquire of the Lord to see if judgment was indeed coming upon them. The priests then went to Huldah, a recognized prophetess living in the capital of Jerusalem. She confirmed the coming judgment but assured King Josiah that it would not come in his lifetime because he had humbled himself before God and his heart was tender toward the Lord. Then King Josiah took action, made a covenant before God that his kingdom would serve and obey God. He enacted spiritual reform throughout the land, and the land was spared during his lifetime. Huldah's words to the king impacted the nation for a generation, and helped stay God's hand of judgment.

Esther was the second wife of King Xerxes of Persia, whom we are told in Esther 1:1-2, ruled the world from Ethiopia to India, one hundred and twenty-seven provinces in all, from his throne in Susa the capital. The Jews had been enslaved by the Babylonians and exported to Babylon when they conquered the land of Israel. Babylon was later conquered by the Persians. As the account goes, the Jews were going to be slaughtered on the king's edict because of the work of one evil man called Haman. Esther, encouraged by her Uncle Mordecai, courageously petitioned the king on his throne for legislation to prevent the massacre. Esther, unbeknownst to her husband, was Jewish. The king listened to Esther and enacted legislation for the Jews to defend themselves, and Haman was hanged. Thus the nation of Israel was preserved, the Jews eventually went back to Israel to rebuild the capital city of Jerusalem and the Temple, and from an earthly perspective the coming of the Messiah was again assured.

Jeremiah 9:17-21 doesn't speak of a specific woman, but of **women associated with the capital city of Jerusalem**. It is a call to mourn, weep, lament, and intercede before God on the city's behalf in the face of certain coming judgment for the nation's sins. *"Call for the wailing women…"* God said, and *"teach your daughters wailing…"*. As professional mourners were hired at funerals to proclaim that a great grief had befallen a family, so God wanted Israel to know that a great grief was about to befall the city. In the same way God calls women everywhere to weep and pray and intercede for their nations in the face of national sins grievous to God. God's nature is to pardon sin, and or to postpone judgment for a generation when there is intercession on behalf of a nation (Exodus 32:32; Numbers 14:19; 1 Kings 8:30; 39; 2 Chronicles 6:21; 2 Chronicles 7:14). God says women are to teach their daughters to pray because they will impact subsequent generations. Women, we have a call from God to pray for our capitols and for our state and national leadership, and we have the mandate to teach our daughters to do the same. By impacting governments through prayer, we impact our families and our societies, and the church is able to exist peacefully in society for generations to come until the Lord's return (1 Timothy 2:1-4).

Anna is the fourth and last prophetess mentioned by name in Scripture, and she is found in the New Testament, Luke 2:36-38. We find that she was committed to fasting and praying for her nation in the Temple in the capital city of Jerusalem. She was from the tribe of Asher, was then about eighty-four years old and had been a widow for many years. Like Simeon, who is recorded in the text immediately prior to this passage as "*looking for the consolation of Israel*", she was "*looking for redemption in Jerusalem*". In other words the desire expressed in her prayers was for God to hasten the sending of the promised Messiah to redeem His people. To these two aged prayer warriors the Lord granted the privilege of seeing the fulfillment of their prayers and of the Lord's long-promised Messiah, the King of kings and Lord of lords, for they saw that very Babe in the arms of Joseph and Mary when taken to the Temple by his parents to be dedicated. Anna then proclaimed what she had witnessed to all who, like her, were looking expectantly in faith for the Messiah's arrival

Lydia, whom we meet in Acts 16:14-15, was the first gentile known to come to Christ in Europe under Paul's ministry, and she was also a woman. She lived and worked in Philippi, the former capital city in Macedonia, and she opened her home to the Gospel ministry once saved. Philippi was a Roman colony, a very privileged status for provincial cities, and a city strategic to Paul's plan. Lydia was a prominent businesswoman from Thyatira who had expanded her business to Philippi. She sold *"purple goods"*. Thyatira was famous for its expensive purple dyes used in coloring the textiles and clothing of the rich and famous, and so we can gather that her business was with the rich, the nobility, and the influential political leaders of the city. Lydia was a prayer warrior, participated in the founding of the church at Philippi, was part of a group of women prayer warriors, in a prominent, strategic city, and would have been influential in praying for and influencing its leadership with the gospel.

We meet **Pricilla** in Acts 18:1-3, 18-19, 24-28 (also Romans 16:3; 1 Corinthians 16:19; and 2 Timothy 4:19), who together with her husband Aquila owned a tent-making business. After their conversion, the two became co-laborers of Paul establishing house churches in strategic capitals of the Roman Empire, and they were well known among the churches for their work. They are mentioned six different times in the New Testament, so they figure prominently in the early work of the spread of the gospel. They were true ministry partners. We meet them first in

Corinth, the capital city of the province of Achaia, twice in Rome, the imperial capital of the Roman Empire, and last in Ephesus laboring with Timothy in that capital city. The highway systems the Romans built throughout their empire expedited the spread of the gospel during that first century A.D. and early on it reached the shores of Britain. As someone who was born and raised in England with its legacy of church and missions, I for one am grateful for the work of Pricilla in using her home in Rome for the work of the gospel. I look forward to meeting her and thanking her!

The Biblical Imperative

When we read Daniel chapter 10, especially verses 13 and 21, together with Isaiah 14:12-14, and Ezekiel 28:12-15, we find that Satan has the similar goal and strategy of reaching the capitals of the world, but for his own evil ends. Satan was created by God as one of the anointed cherubim, possibly the third archangel along with Michael and Gabriel, but he became full of pride and set about usurping the throne of God. We know that Satan will never achieve his ends, and that God's power is greater than Satan's power, but these Scriptures give us the imperative to work in prayer as Daniel did to prevent Satan from gaining control of the world's capitals, or to wrest control of them from him. Paul understood this for in Ephesians 6:12 he says, "*For we wrestle not against flesh and blood but against principalities, against powers, against the rulers of the darkness of this world, against spiritual wickedness in high places*"(Principalities are areas over which a prince rules). The four entities listed in that Ephesians' verse are also the four foes of the church. And that reminds us of Paul's exhortation in 1 Timothy 2:1-4 to pray first for, "*kings and all those in authority...that we* [the church] *might live quiet and peaceable lives...*" (emphasis mine). Also, in Nehemiah 6:7-14 we find that there are women on the enemy's side in the battle for capitals. A false prophetess named **Noadiah** was hired to work against Nehemiah in the work of rebuilding the broken walls of the capital city of Jerusalem, so that it stayed squarely in the hands of the enemy. Noadiah did not succeed. Nehemiah was not deterred but rather, determined to finish the work, which he did. If at the very beginning Satan attempted to wrest control of earth by targeting Eve, we must not be surprised that he beguiles women to be on his side in the battle still today.

The Kingdom Commission to Women

Putting together Jeremiah 9:17-21, 1 Timothy 2:1-4, and the biblical examples, we find that God calls women to pray for their nation's leadership, and especially engage in battle in prayer for them, and even to find opportunities to share the gospel with them. It is God's will that the political leadership of nations will be saved. The resulting influence of Christian kings and political leadership is that the church and Christians live quiet and peaceful lives in their communities, free to share the gospel in every level of society without hindrance. In the book of Philippians we find that Paul reached the Roman Praetorian guard for Christ, and subsequently many in Caesar's household came to Christ, too (Philippians 1:13, 4:22). That freedom to share needs to be exercised.

We need to be proactive and organized as women because God is using us and will use our daughters to thwart the enemy's plans and remove his strongholds through prayer. Indiana as a state is an example of the fact that God does indeed put godly people in positions of power. It is an encouragement to continue to pray for our state and nation. We don't want death in our windows and our children slain; we want to live quiet and peaceable lives, raising our families for God, free to share the gospel, enjoying the blessing of this life, until Christ's return to rule and reign.

Pamela Russell
Capitol Commission
Indiana Director of Women's Ministries